Identity Interconnections

ACPA BOOKS AND MEDIA CONTACT INFORMATION

ACPA International Office
Tricia A. Fechter Gates
Deputy Executive Director
One Dupont Circle NW, Suite 300
Washington, DC 20036-1110
(202) 759-4825
pfechter@acpa.nche.edu

ACPA Publications Board
Mimi Benjamin, Co-Editor
Professor
Indiana University of Pennsylvania
Stouffer Hall, Room 206
1175 Maple Street
Indiana, PA 15705
mbenjami@iup.edu

Jody E. Jessup-Anger, Co-Editor
Professor
Marquette University
PO Box 1881
Milwaukee, WI 53201
Jody.jessup-anger@marquette.edu

Identity Interconnections

Pursuing Poststructural Possibilities in Student Affairs Praxis

Edited by
AERIEL A. ASHLEE AND
LISA DELACRUZ COMBS

Foreword by
MARC P. JOHNSTON-GUERRERO

Afterword by
ELISA S. ABES

ACPA
College Student
Educators International

STERLING, VIRGINIA

Published by Stylus Publishing, LLC.
22883 Quicksilver Drive
Sterling, Virginia 20166-2019

Library of Congress Cataloging-in-Publication-Data
The CIP data for this title is forthcoming.

13-digit ISBN: 978-1-64267-344-9 (cloth)
13-digit ISBN: 978-1-64267-345-6 (paperback)
13-digit ISBN: 978-1-64267-346-3 (library networkable e-edition)
13-digit ISBN: 978-1-64267-347-0 (consumer e-edition)

Printed in the United States of America

All first editions printed on acid free paper
that meets the American National Standards Institute
Z39-48 Standard.

Bulk Purchases

Quantity discounts are available for use in workshops and
for staff development.

Call 1-800-232-0223

First Edition, 2022

Contents

Foreword

As I finished reading this volume, I felt complete awe thinking about all the possibilities within our field. The concept of identity interconnections holds so much promise to bridge different identities, epistemologies, theories, and practice. And I am honored to be able to witness the evolution of an idea that partially started with my thinking about the comparability of different identities, then to a shared consideration of analogies and metaphors across identities, and now to the editors' focus on identity interconnections. In this volume, Aeriel and Lisa have generated a community of knowledge contributors and innovative practitioners all centered around this important line of thinking. And I want to point out that this cultivation of community began well before the call for proposals went out for this book.

In 2017, Aeriel put together an interactive symposium presented at the Association for the Study of Higher Education (ASHE) Annual Conference in Houston, Texas. It was titled, "One of These Things Is Not Like the Other": Using Identity Analogies and Metaphors in Higher Education, and included myself and the two coeditors, along with Z Nicolazzo, D-L Stewart, and Vu Tran. We continued the community building in June of 2018 by presenting a follow-up session at the National Conference on Race and Ethnicity (NCORE). That session added Alandis A. Johnson and Stephen Deaderick and was titled, "It's Sort of Like . . .": Using Identity Analogies and Metaphors in Higher Education. The first session took a more critical approach to identity analogies while the second session tried to think more expansively about the potential benefits of their usage. I share these details because I want to preface that the coeditors' thinking on this topic has a strong foundation and we can even track the evolution of their ideas from identity analogies to identity interconnections.

The fields of higher education and student affairs are ripe for this evolution of thinking, particularly with the recent and prominent examples of White academics (faculty and graduate students) taking on minoritized racial and ethnic identities that aren't their own. What is it about the systems and structures of higher education that perhaps encouraged these fraudulent identities in the first place? How can theory help us not only better understand the power dynamics at play, but also how we might move forward? Based on the chapters in this volume, I believe identity interconnections are a key to being able to answer these questions and so many more that continue to evade higher education practitioners.

As the editors situate this volume in the third wave of student development theories given its poststructural leaning, I wonder if it's actually more of a bridge to what might be a fourth wave, or perhaps just clearer distinction between critical and poststructural theorizing within the third wave. In any case, this volume serving as a bridge is clear in many aspects, like bridging identity analogies to identity interconnections and bridging the social identities many of us hold onto tightly and the potential for no longer needing those constraining categories.

To this point I want to highlight the importance of the editors' caution in their introduction. Identity interconnectivity could easily be critiqued because like other poststructural theories, there is a tension between the identities and categories we have found useful for framing our experience, and the potential for dismantling the systems that would prevent us from having those marginalizing experiences in the first place. The contributors to this volume are offering readers entryways for better understanding across identities, by going through the critical perspectives and honoring the marginalizing experiences so many of us have had in life and within higher education specifically. These experiences cannot be overlooked, and I am so appreciative that many chapters seamlessly weave narratives and theorizing together, all to inform implications for practice.

I want to honor the volume's focus on practice. As a former student affairs educator, turned faculty, and now an academic administrator, I can attest to the radical potential for this work to truly transform our practice, and I so appreciated the ways the chapters intentionally engaged practice in multiple forms. Moreover, the breadth of the landscape of different identities engaged within the volume is impressive. Yes, not all identities are covered, but that would be impossible in one volume! The promise of interconnectivity is that we don't have to cover everything here and now. The learning that occurs from these specific identity interconnections can be used and translated toward further interconnections.

The editors of this volume have inspiringly offered us the bridge we have been missing, and I cannot wait to see what is on the other side.

Marc P. Johnston-Guerrero
The Ohio State University

Acknowledgments

This book is a manifestation of interconnectivity and embodies the expansive possibilities that can arise from pursuing commonalities that do not diminish difference, but rather recognize our radical interrelatedness and inspire listening with an openness to be changed by what we hear. First, we thank our 13 amazing contributing authors. This book is only possible because of their willingness to imaginatively and collaboratively explore identity interconnections with us. We are humbled and deeply grateful for their vulnerability, innovation, and belief in the healing and liberatory potential of poststructural praxis in student affairs. We also thank Elisa S. Abes for planting seeds and inviting us to pursue poststructural wondering related to student affairs and higher education during our graduate studies at Miami University (Ohio). We thank Marc P. Johnston-Guerrero, Vu Tran, Z Nicolazzo, D-L Stewart, Alandis A. Johnson, and Stephen Deaderick for contributing to earlier iterations of this project, including a 2017 Association for the Study of Higher Education interactive symposium that clarified for us the importance of engaging identity interconnections with compassionate caution and a 2018 session at the National Conference on Race and Ethnicity that confirmed the ubiquity of identity interconnections and cemented for us the need for this book. We thank AnaLouise Keating (who we first encountered through Gloria Anzaldúa's writing) who served as a guidepost for our theoretical framing. We thank our mentors Marc P. Johnston-Guerrero and Stephen John Quaye for believing in us and encouraging us to believe in ourselves and the value of our ideas. We thank Kyle C. Ashlee for spending countless hours thinking with us, helping us to refine identity interconnections, and providing thoughtful feedback on early drafts of the project. We also thank Mimi Benjamin and Jody Jessup-Anger, the ACPA Books series editors, for their support of us, this project, and their mentorship throughout the editing process. Finally, we express profound gratitude for the incredible

xi

learning and growing we experienced together in the process of conceptualizing and editing this book. Identity interconnections first grew out of a coffee date and shared desire to connect with and through our racialized stories of (un)belonging; that we found healing, connection, and opportunities for aspiring allyship through our own identity interconnections is a gift beyond words.

Aeriel thanks her first/birth, adopted, and chosen family for the indelible impact they have made on her way of thinking, being, and moving through the world. Aeriel is profoundly grateful to her husband, Kyle C. Ashlee, who has been a tireless champion of her thinking and writing. Last, but certainly not least, Aeriel thanks her amazing 3-and-a-half-year-old daughter, Azaelea Grace Ashlee, for sharing her joy, laughter, and childlike wonder; and for tugging at mommy's pant leg gently reminding her to close her computer and come play.

Lisa thanks her family for encouraging her dreams to be filled with expansive thinking and love. She also thanks her partner, Ryan, for keeping her grounded and supporting her throughout this project. Lastly, Lisa thanks her mentors Aeriel, Stephen, and Marc for believing in her and pushing her thinking and ideas.

Introduction

Aeriel A. Ashlee and Lisa Delacruz Combs

A connectionist approach can be vital during times of fragmentation. When we view conflicts from connectionist perspectives, we try to look beneath surface judgements, rigid labels, and other divisive ways of thinking. We seek commonalities and move toward healing. (Keating, 2013, p. 17)

As student affairs educators, we believe that theory has the power to heal and transform individuals and institutions. In particular, we have been encouraged and inspired by the growing body of scholarship exploring the potential of critical and poststructural theoretical frameworks in college student development (Abes et al., 2019). By questioning, resisting, and unlearning inherited systems of power, poststructural frameworks invite expansive possibilities for liberation and social transformation (Ashlee & Ashlee, 2022). Yet, the troubling dichotomy of theory versus practice persists in student affairs (Blimling, 2011). Even as momentum has grown in the theoretical exploration of critical and poststructural perspectives in higher education (Abes, 2016), there continues to be a gap in translating those theories into student affairs practice. This book aims to address that gap by introducing *identity interconnections* as a purposeful process of integrating poststructural theory and student affairs practice. Drawing from Freire's (1993) notion of *praxis*—engaging reflection and action for transformation—identity interconnections invite intentional *reflection* on affective relating across identities to foster expansive considerations of commonalities and differences as sites for deepening identity development and social justice *action*. In other words, identity interconnections offer practical possibilities for how poststructural

1

theory, namely interconnectivity (Keating, 2013), can transform student affairs in higher education.

In our years of professional experience in student affairs and higher education, we have regularly observed students and colleagues draw parallels between identity experiences. From informal conversations in identity-based student organizations to intellectual debates in master's program classrooms to colleagues making connections between national conference presentations, we have repeatedly witnessed individuals make comparisons across identity groups as a meaning-making process. Tran and Johnston-Guerrero (2016) refer to this practice as "an identity analogy," which they describe as "analogizing one identity or one group's experience to help individuals understand another" (p. 134). While exploring similarities across identities can be a useful catalyst for multicultural education (Tran & Johnston-Guerrero, 2016), without acknowledging differences between identities and without situating identity experiences in inherited systems of power, this practice can problematically perpetuate ideas of sameness and minimize the very tangible ways inherited systems of power differentially affect distinct groups.

For example, this may occur when undergraduate student leaders liken the disclosure of an invisible disability with "coming out" as LGBTQ+ but fail to examine how ableism and heterosexism operate differently. Another example might be when graduate students compare monoracial passing to passing as heterosexual without carefully considering the nuances of multiple intersecting identities, thus rendering individuals who are multiracial and queer invisible. Even as student affairs professional networks form around shared racialized experiences—for example, the ACPA Multiracial Network and the NASPA Transracial Adoptee and Multiracial Knowledge Community—unless this type of coalition building is undertaken with concurrent investigations of monoracism, the unique system of oppression that targets individuals who do not fit into monoracial categories or groups (Johnston & Nadal, 2010), and account for the ways in which biological kinship is privileged over adoptive family formations, these efforts may be reductionist at best.

In addition to examining points of difference, student affairs educators must attend to the systemic implications of examining similarities between identities as an ethical and pedagogical imperative. This is where the tendency to draw similarities across identities as a meaning-making practice must be intentionally connected to and grounded in theory that situates lived experiences within inherited systems of power. It is our hope that by naming identity interconnections as an intentional student affairs praxis, we can encourage student affairs educators to ground and connect identity analogies (Tran & Johnston-Guerrero, 2016) in theory that accounts for inherited systems of power.

THRESHOLD THEORIZING

In seeking to bridge the disconnect between the growing cannon of critical and poststructural theories with contemporary student affairs practice, we turn to the notion of threshold theorizing. Keating (2013) describes threshold theories as "nonbinary, liminal, potentially transformative" (p. 10) approaches to thinking and being. Liminality is existing beyond boundaries in the both/and of in-between spaces, occupying a middle ground (Turner, 1969). As two Womxn of Color who know intimately the power and potential of liminal positionalities (as a transracial adoptee and multiracial person, respectively) we were immediately intrigued by the possibilities of threshold theorizing for this project. By our very racial embodiment, we experience both/and: Aeriel is both an Asian American Adoptee of Color and someone raised in and socialized by a White adoptive family. Lisa is both Asian American, Filipina and White. Furthermore, as student affairs scholar-practitioners seeking to nuance and complicate the persistent disconnect between theory and practice, we found Keating's theory of interconnectivity well situated to inform student affairs praxis (Ashlee & Ashlee, 2022).

According to Keating (2013), oppositional approaches to education and identity have not been effective in producing long-term change or radically healing and transforming society. The current rigid categorical structures prevalent in U.S. culture—and reflected in higher education—are limited because they create boxes that are perceived to be discrete, thus limiting ways of knowing and inhibiting ways of relating. In Keating's words,

> Most (if not all) of us educated in western school systems have been trained to think in disconnectionist terms, to look for the differences (defined narrowly) between our views and those of others, and to heighten these differences while ignoring possible points of connection. (p. 7)

To be clear, we are not suggesting the minimization of race, gender, or other socially constructed categories by which resources are inequitably and unjustly distributed. Rather, we invite an interrogation of inherited systems of power that shapes socially constructed identity categories in the first place in order to radically and expansively envision and work toward more liberatory futures.

Threshold theories are inherently relational (Keating, 2013). As such, we want to make plain our relationship to each other and the threshold theory that informs the framing of this book. We (Aeriel and Lisa) both identify as Asian American Womxn of Color; yet we have both long battled with questions of racial belonging given our transracial adoptee and multiracial identities. Early in our friendship, we began comparing anecdotes of marginalization and exotification due to the ways our racialized experiences (while distinctly different) have similarly defied the rigidity imposed by essentialized definitions of race. Through sharing and deeply listening to each other's stories, we developed a kinship around our shared experience of "not feeling racially enough" (Ashlee & Quaye, 2020, p. 2). This connection has been healing and catalytic for our own identity development.

Moreover, exploring the differences in our experiences as a transracial adoptee and multiracial person respectively, has enabled us to interrogate broader systems of power (such as monoracism and the privileging of biological kinship over adoptive family formations). Thus, what began as an exploration of similarities between our identities led to critically examining differences across our experiences framed within a systems lens. By naming and recognizing our respective points of privilege (and how we may be complicit in each other's oppression), we have become better allies for one another. Thus, our story serves as an example of and an entry point to interconnectivity (Keating, 2013) as a threshold theory with healing and transformative potential.

UNDERSTANDING INTERCONNECTIVITY

Informed by the writing and thinking of Womxn of Color (Anzaldúa & Keating, 2002; Moraga & Anzaldúa, 1981), Keating's (2013) theorizing of interconnectivity—which is the framework for this edited volume—invites readers to consider how power plays out (similarly and differently) across socially constructed identity groups. In her book, *Transformation Now! Toward a Post-Oppositional Politics of Change*, Keating (2013) outlines three theoretical contributions, which offer compelling considerations for students, scholars, and activists seeking to foster social justice across diverse positionalities and perspectives.

The first lesson of interconnectivity is to seek commonalities by making connections through difference (Keating, 2013). Evoking an expansive way of thinking and relating, Keating's call for pursuing commonalities does not diminish difference but rather "redefines difference in potentially transform-ative ways" (p. 38). Grounded in a hermeneutics of love, the commonali-ties which Keating invites us to consider are not to be reduced to assertions of sameness. Rather, Keating's commonalities are expansive enough to hold similarities and differences in tension with one another, beckoning a critical analysis of both as pathways for identity development, coalition building, and social justice action.

The second lesson of interconnectivity is to examine our radical inter-relatedness (Keating, 2013). According to Keating, recognizing that we are interconnected (intrapersonally and interpersonally) has "concrete ethical implications" (p. 49) from which an ethical imperative of accountability emerges. No matter how different, distant, or divided current events, people, and perspectives might be, our actions—and thus our accountability to one another—are intricately intertwined. This lens of interrelatedness requires a relational (rather than solely oppositional) approach to knowing and being.

The third lesson of interconnectivity is to listen with raw openness (Keating, 2013). Akin to cultural and intellectual humility (Foronda et al., 2016), Keating explains that this "deep, self-reflective listening takes tremen-dous effort, demands vulnerability, and requires a willingness to be altered by the words spoken" (p. 52). Inherent to this final theoretical contribution of interconnectivity is recognizing the emotionally complex nature of this praxis. By remaining receptive to learning the limitations of our own per-spective, we open ourselves to the possibilities of growth and greater connec-tion with others.

Through pursuing complex commonalities expansive enough to hold both similarities and differences, student affairs educators can ethically consider identity interconnections in such a way that does not problematically diminish difference, but instead recognizes points of difference as opportunities for social justice action. By pursuing radical interconnectivity, student affairs educators can advance an interdependent understanding of inherited systems of power, recognizing the ways in which all systems (and thus all oppression, and all liberation) are interconnected. This interconnected insight can enable student affairs educators to extend beyond binary and oppositional thinking, and in turn, give rise to the formation of new coalitions. Finally, by listening with raw openness (allowing ourselves, and encouraging our students, to be changed by others' experiences), student affairs educators can facilitate identity development and social justice action as interrelated endeavors.

IDENTITY INTERCONNECTIONS AS A
PRAXIS OF INTERCONNECTIVITY

This book presents a compilation of identity interconnections as a praxis—a process of reflection and action—of interconnectivity (Keating, 2013) in student affairs and higher education. By reflecting on commonalities across diverse identities, we hope student affairs educators can contribute to a liberatory future. Through sharing stories of identity development, vulnerably and expansively connecting across and between socially constructed categories, we hope student affairs educators (and the students with whom we work) can begin recognizing our radical interrelatedness. By interrogating common constructs such as liminality, authenticity, temporality, and dominance, we hope student affairs educators can listen with the intent to be changed, connecting to and learning with one another across identities in order to build coalitions, take social justice action, and transform higher education.

Identity interconnections are grounded in an ethical imperative, a call of accountability, which we refer to as *compassionate caution*. We define compassionate caution as an empathetic application of identity interconnections, which involves a deliberate examination of both similarities and differences across identities and an acknowledgment of how inherited systems of power inform different positionalities. Compassionate caution is etched right into the framework of interconnectivity and requires intentionality when employing identity interconnections in praxis. For example, to engage identity interconnections with compassionate caution necessitates both an examination of similarities (as sites for coalition building) and intentional exploration of differences (as the foreground for social justice action). It is not enough to only consider commonalities (such as analogizing across identities); identity interconnections must also account for points of divergence. This book provides concrete examples for how to engage identity interconnections with compassionate caution so that student affairs educators can explore identity interconnections in ways that do not signify sameness (thereby minimizing very real differences in and between identity experiences), but rather facilitate interconnectivity in ways that disrupt inherited systems of power.

THE POSSIBILITIES OF POSTSTRUCTURALISM
IN STUDENT AFFAIRS

As poststructural scholars, we are often asked how abstract concepts associated with critical and poststructural theories can be applied to student affairs practice. We offer identity interconnections as an answer to that question and as a pedagogical praxis that can be utilized by student affairs educators. Having a poststructural worldview is an extension of the critical paradigm where systems of power are named, and the focus is on deconstruction, imagination, and pursuing expansive ways of thinking that move beyond the rigid and binary (Abes, 2016). As a praxis of interconnectivity (Keating, 2013), identity interconnections assert that social identities matter (grounded in a critical framework) and that they do not have to define or dictate possibilities for the future. As feminist author, poet, and activist Audre Lorde (2007) wrote, we must learn "how to take our differences and make them strengths. *For the master's tools will never dismantle the master's house*" (p. 112). Rather than adhering to or complying with inherited power structures, poststructuralism invites us to let go of that which does not serve us and (re)learn to trust ourselves, our intuition, and our ways of knowing, being, and relating. Identity interconnections (re)imagine the master's tools as a departure from dominant ways of knowing and being to offer a new approach that centers poststructural perspectives through relational and post-oppositional thinking, informed by Womxn of Color theorizing (Keating, 2013; Moraga & Anzaldúa, 2015).

In full transparency, sometimes the path of pursuing poststructural possibilities in student affairs has been challenging at times; indeed, blazing new trails often is. And, we have remained steadfast by remembering that this is not a solitary pursuit. We hope that by summoning the courage to write these words, and by featuring student affairs scholars and practitioners who have firsthand experience with identity interconnections, that we can invite others to explore poststructural possibilities in student affairs praxis. Interrogating the limiting and limited nature of dominant conceptualizations of social identity, diversity, and difference requires (re)imagining power, which is not an easy task. And, it is one we undertake in earnest, as we (like others who have come before us) believe that theory can be healing and transformative (Jones & Stewart, 2016).

A project of third-wave student development theory (Jones & Stewart, 2016), this book explores the liberatory possibilities of Keating's (2013) poststructural theory of interconnectivity in student affairs praxis. Each chapter explores and examines experiences that bind us, interconnections across and between diverse positionalities and perspectives.

ORGANIZATION OF THE BOOK

The chapters of this book are aligned, both in content and layout, with our expansive, poststructural worldview, symbolically and tangibly manifesting interconnectivity. Too often, the world and higher education are situated in oppositional terms: Black versus White, happy versus sad, early versus late, and so on. Moreover, higher education and student affairs is often segmented along false dichotomies of theory versus practice and scholar versus practitioner, when in actuality, the relationship between the two is far more nuanced and requires a complex integration of both. This book presents 10 examples of reimagining dichotomies of difference while exploring commonalities as sites for identity development and social justice action. Informed by a poststructural lens grounded in interconnectivity (Keating, 2013), the chapters provide theoretical analysis, personal narratives, and professional implications for fostering connections through difference, exploring radical interrelatedness, and listening with raw openness to engage identity interconnections as an expansive approach to identity development and social justice action in student affairs and higher education.

To start, Duran discusses how identity interconnections can inform and innovate how we engage theory in student affairs when undertaken with responsible stewardship. Next, Campa explores the intrapersonal implications of identity interconnections as a multiracial and interfaith individual. By sharing her personal narrative of navigating liminality within her own identity development, she thoughtfully invites student affairs educators to consider the power of expansive language in constructing social identities that challenge binary thinking. In chapter 3, Bui shares her story of voice, examining accents across national borders and different abilities to illustrate how interconnectivity can facilitate connection and empathy across diverse identities. Johnson then draws interconnections across theories of gender and ability in chapter 4 to demonstrate how fluidity and an expanded understanding of identity can offer post-oppositional possibilities for student affairs practice. In chapter 5, Risku explores identity interconnections between multiracial and trans* identities, reflecting on the ways radical interrelatedness can spark social justice action. Then follows Bettencourt who offers an analysis of identity interconnections from a practitioner lens, in chapter 6, describing how disclosure can be a powerful praxis of interconnectivity that enables educators to better serve and support working-class students and students with disabilities.

In chapter 7, Cepeda and Prieto explore identity interconnections between biracial and bisexual people as sites for solidarity between and across diverse communities. Next, K. Ashlee and Cash explore how the identity interconnection between masculinity and whiteness can be a tool for developing critical consciousness and inspiring social justice action. Sasaki offers, in chapter 9, an example of how identity interconnections can (re)shape how educators think about and structure student affairs by sharing the creation story of an Asian Pacific Islander Middle Eastern Desi American services office. Finally, in chapter 10, Rivera and Wallace offer cautionary tales of intersectional erasure to convey the importance of engaging identity interconnections with compassionate caution and intentionality.

This book seeks to nuance the complexities of both/and by illuminating how poststructural perspectives of relating across differences and similarities may start to blur the lines between theory and practice. Identity interconnections as a praxis of interconnectivity (Keating, 2013) are an alternative path to historic dichotomies of theory versus practice and us versus them. As poststructural scholars, we have been pushed on the practicality and application of poststructural thought to an applied field such as student affairs. We have heard comments like, "This is all great in theory, but how can student affairs practitioners actually apply this?" It is our hope that this book helps to answer that question by providing a theoretical framework and multiple practical examples for employing identity interconnections as an expansive approach to identity development and social justice action in student affairs and higher education.

REFERENCES

Abes, E. S. (Ed.). (2016). *Critical perspectives on student development theory* (New Directions for Student Services, no. 154). Jossey-Bass.

Abes, E. S., Jones, S. R., & Stewart, D. L. (Eds.). (2019). *Rethinking college student development theory using critical frameworks*. Stylus.

Anzaldúa, G. (1987). *Borderlands/La frontera: The new mestiza*. Aunt Lute Books.

Anzaldúa, G., & Keating, A. (Eds.) (2002). *this bridge we call home: radical visions for transformation*. Routledge.

Ashlee, K. C., & Ashlee, A. A. (2022). A critical praxis of interconnectivity in student affairs. In S. B. Marine & C. Gilbert (Eds.), *Critical praxis in higher education and student affairs: Social justice in action* (pp. 88–103). Stylus.

Ashlee, A. A., & Quaye, S. J. (2020). On being racially enough: A duoethnography across minoritized racial identities. *International Journal of Qualitative Studies in Education, 34*(3), 243–261. https://doi.org/10.1080/09518398.2020.1753256

Blimling, G. S. (2011). How are dichotomies such as scholar/practitioner and theory/practice helpful and harmful to the profession? Developing professional judgment. In P. M. Magolda & M. B. Baxter Magolda (Eds.), *Contested issues in student affairs: Diverse perspectives and respectful dialogue* (pp. 42–53). Stylus.

Foronda, C., Baptiste, D. L., Reinholdt, M. M., & Ousman, K. (2016). Cultural humility: A concept analysis. *Journal of Transcultural Nursing, 27*(3), 210–217. https://doi.org/10.1177/1043659615592677

Freire, P. (1993). *Pedagogy of the oppressed.* Bloomsbury.

Johnston, M., & Nadal, K. (2010). Multiracial microaggressions. In D. W. Sue (Ed.), *Microaggressions and marginality: Manifestation, dynamics, and impact* (pp. 123–144). Wiley.

Jones, S. R., & Stewart, D. L. (2016). Evolution of student development theory. In E. S. Abes (Ed.), *Critical perspectives on student development theory* (New Directions for Student Services, no. 154, pp. 17–28). Jossey-Bass. https://doi.org/10.1002/ss.20172

Keating, A. (2013). *Transformation now! Toward a post-oppositional politics of change.* University of Illinois Press.

Lorde, A. (1984). *Sister/outsider.* Crossing Press.

Moraga, C., & Anzaldúa, G. (Eds.). (1981). *This bridge called my back: Writings by radical women of color.* Persephone Press.

Tran, V. T., & Johnston-Guerrero, M. P. (2016). Is transracial the same as transgender? The utility and limitations of identity analogies in multicultural education. *Multicultural Perspectives, 18*(3), 134–139. https://doi.org/10.1080/15210960.2016.1186548

Turner, V. (1969). *The ritual process: Structure and anti-structure.* Aldine.

1

Exploring Responsible Stewardship of Identity Interconnections in Student Development Theorizing

Antonio Duran

SUPPORTING THE HOLISTIC DEVELOPMENT of students has long been a defining feature of the student affairs profession (Patton et al., 2016). In particular, scholars have argued that the college environment serves as a meaningful context for students to broach questions related to identity, morals, knowledge creation, and navigating relationships. In an attempt to learn how to assist students in their development, student affairs educators frequently reference theories developed within and outside of the field of higher education (e.g., psychology, social psychology, and sociology; Jones & Abes, 2013; Patton et al., 2016; Torres et al., 2009). From there, professionals attempt to mobilize these formal bodies of theories within their institutional contexts, asking what it means to translate this knowledge to their practice (Reason & Kimball, 2012). Thus, it is unsurprising that leading student affairs professional organizations maintain that understanding students' development and learning is key to the field (ACPA & NASPA, 2015).

And still, the study of student development theory has continued to shift, grow, and evolve in recent years (Torres et al., 2019). In fact, one of the most noteworthy developments in this area of study is the use of critical and poststructural theories to reimagine what student affairs educators think of when they conceptualize matters of development (Abes, 2016;

Jones & Stewart, 2016). Referred to as the third wave of student development, researchers have started to understand how systems of power and oppression influence students' developmental realities (Abes et al., 2019; Jones & Stewart, 2016). Additionally, this third wave has moved beyond relying on traditional theoretical understandings that typically relied on concepts such as stages, phases, vectors, or positions. Instead, one of the interventions of the third wave is that it invites student affairs scholars and educators alike to comprehend central constructs of development that may be present across students' experiences (Abes et al., 2019).

It is in this third wave that I situate my exploration of the potential that identity interconnections hold for student affairs educators' ability to support students in their development. Specifically, I enter this conversation on identity interconnections and interconnectivity (Keating, 2013), seeking to analyze how identity interconnections can be a useful way to think through how to apply theoretical frameworks and constructs across social identity groups. Additionally, throughout this chapter, I am influenced by Keating's (2013) writing on interconnectivity, noting how the third wave inherently bridges different types of analysis in the hopes of exposing how power and oppression shape development broadly. In the process of doing so, I argue that student affairs educators should be responsible stewards of identity interconnections when used in the context of student development theorizing, referencing the idea of stewardship introduced by theorists who worry about the misappropriation of specific ideas and frameworks (e.g., Hancock, 2016; Moradi & Grzanka, 2017). Specifically, I begin by providing some brief remarks on the study of student development theory, focusing on how the third wave has advanced this area of research. Next, I offer an example vignette of how identity interconnections may lend themselves to student development theory, before outlining specific points of relevance. I conclude by articulating explicit recommendations for student affairs educators.

GUIDING PERSPECTIVES ON STUDENT DEVELOPMENT THEORY

The focus of the student affairs field on student development has been around since the first half of the 20th century, with formative documents published on the value of attending to the whole student emerging in the 1930s (see American Council on Education, 1937/1994). This commitment to playing a role in students' development was subsequently affirmed in the 1970s with the publication of such works like *Student Development in Tomorrow's Higher Education* (Brown, 1972). It was also around the 1960s and 1970s that theorists began to conduct research on specific domains of development (e.g., psychosocial, cognitive, moral). Though not frequently conducted with the specific interest of the college years, this body of knowledge paved the way for future research attentive to the college environment.

In an attempt to capture the wide breadth of knowledge that has emerged about college student development, Jones and Stewart (2016) borrowed the language of "waves," which scholars have used to describe feminist thought. In their conceptualization of the waves of student development, Jones and Stewart (2016) asserted that three are currently in existence. The first wave most commonly encapsulates the theories that first started to appear in the 1960s and 1970s. Although formative to the field's understandings of college students, these theories frequently isolated development into specific domains and largely relied on privileged populations as the basis for this research (e.g., White, straight, cisgender men and women). The second wave was pivotal to challenging the student affairs profession on how development can be more complex than previously understood and also opened up an interest in social identities. In particular, second wave scholars showed how domains of development could influence one another (referred to as integrative approaches). Moreover, the second wave demonstrated a focus on minoritized groups broadly, including theories that explained how people came to view and relate to their social identities (e.g., race, gender, sexuality). Though this area of research acknowledged the social construction of identities, theorists failed to implicate the role that systems of power play in shaping identity development.

It is in the third wave that researchers resist power-neutral perspectives on student development theory. Specifically, third wave scholars see an imperative to conceptualize how structures of inequity inform the developmental tasks that college students face. This aim is accomplished through the use of critical and poststructural theories that exist outside of education including, but not limited to, intersectionality (Crenshaw, 1989), critical race theory (Delgado & Stefancic, 2017), and crip theory (McRuer, 2006). Researchers have applied these theoretical perspectives to shed light on the realities encountered by individuals in college contexts (Abes, 2016; Duran & Jones, 2020; Okello, 2018; Perez, 2019). Additionally, the third wave of student development theory brings into question what scholars and educators consider to be "development." Past waves of student development theory investigated particular domain(s) of development, seeking to understand the trajectories that people undergo to achieve developmental complexity. For instance, how do people go from being cognitively dualistic to considering the plurality of knowledge? However, in their innovative text highlighting the third wave, Abes et al. (2019) asserted that it may be more meaningful to examine specific constructs that may be present across developmental domains and social identities. Examples of these constructs include agency, context, and resilience. The introduction of these constructs into the canon showcases the possibility of comprehending how people are alike in their developmental journeys more than what was previously understood. As a result, the third wave of student development lends itself to thinking through the notion of identity interconnections highlighted in this volume. To further underscore the relationship between the third wave of student development and identity interconnections, I offer a brief vignette detailing questions that may come up in a graduate preparation course.

VIGNETTE DISPLAYING RELATIONSHIP BETWEEN IDENTITY INTERCONNECTIONS AND STUDENT DEVELOPMENT THEORY

In a graduate class titled Student Development Theory in College, students have reached a week focused on sexual identity development. In this class section, they read the foundational work of Dillon et al. (2011), who offered a unifying model of sexual identity development stemming from research across sexualities, including heterosexual and queer individuals. Additionally, the instructor assigned a monograph that provides an analysis of how queer theory challenges existing understandings related to sexual identity and development (Denton, 2016). Students also had the opportunity to read an article about a specific student population, including queer students with disabilities (Miller et al., 2019).

As a way to spark conversation, the faculty member commences the class by asking people to anonymously write down questions that they have based on the readings. Among the responses submitted, a couple stand out to the instructor. In particular, one student wrote, "I'm straight, so I'm a bit unclear how these ideas apply to me. What does queer theory mean for students like me?" Another individual inquired, "I am a bit confused by the argument that was in the article about queer students with disabilities. What does it mean for people to come out twice? Does using the language/concept of coming out to describe disability identity serve to appropriate ideas from the queer community?" Both responses present very real questions that students in a graduate preparation program, as well as full-time student affairs educators, may wonder about as they work through ideas of student development and identity interconnections. The first anonymous note, in particular, presents a person wondering about how theories that emerged from particular populations have broader applicability than may be seen on the surface. The second comment showcases how connections can be made across social identities as it relates to developmental tasks (e.g., identity disclosure in the case of this student's question). Although I return to this vignette at the conclusion of this chapter, I believe it to be a significant jumping off point to discuss the relevance of identity interconnections to student development theorizing in postsecondary education.

THE RELEVANCE OF IDENTITY INTERCONNECTIONS TO STUDENT DEVELOPMENT THEORY

To articulate how identity interconnections can be an appropriate and meaningful concept to employ within the larger student development theory canon, I find it is important first to introduce the idea of stewardship, which is the relationship that people feel to certain forms of theorizing. In particular, most of my scholarly work in postsecondary education has attempted to honor the framework of intersectionality, an analytic that exposes how systems of power and oppression constitute one another to disproportionately affect those with multiple minoritized identities in society (Crenshaw, 1989). And yet, as I explore further as follows, individuals have rendered intersectionality a buzzword, potentially stripping this framework's intent to identify and challenge how systemic inequities manifest in different contexts (Davis, 2008). Therefore, scholars have used the notion of stewardship to honor commitments to the genealogy and origins of a theory while at the same time envisioning new possibilities and potentials for an idea (Hancock, 2016; Moradi & Grzanka, 2017). Throughout the subsequent sections, I attend to the ways that scholars and educators can be good stewards of student development theory as they consider applying identity interconnections in their work. I begin by articulating the power of applying critical and poststructural frameworks across different populations and emphasizing the potential to think about developmental constructs as a form of applying identity interconnections. I conclude by providing some notes for responsible stewardship, especially as it relates to student development theory.

APPLYING CRITICAL AND POSTSTRUCTURAL
FRAMEWORKS ACROSS POPULATIONS

Integral to third-wave student development theorizing is the mobilization of critical and poststructural perspectives that seek to identify and dismantle how systems of power and oppression manifest in society (Jones & Stewart, 2016). Importantly, these frameworks are applied in ways that bring new understandings about how oppressive realities shape people's developmental complexity. And yet, an interesting phenomenon that frequently occurs is discussions about to whom these theories can and cannot be applied. For instance, is intersectionality only pertinent to examine the lives of Black women, an argument that has been brought up in the past (Nash, 2008)? Does queer theory solely concern the experiences of queer individuals? These types of questions frequently reflect surface-level understandings of these frameworks, constraining the potential of these theories to truly critique oppressive systems.

In reality, these theories are less concerned with people's individual experiences and are more apt to interrogate the systems that shape people's lives. In the case of intersectionality, Chun et al. (2013) posited that it "concerns the way things work rather than who people are" (p. 923), meaning that the defining characteristic of the theory is an interrogation of systems, and who it applies to should be thought about in more expansive ways. Similarly, queer theorists are well positioned to broadly investigate structures such as heteronormativity (Denton, 2016), a set of ideologies and norms that affect all individuals—though the degree to which they do is based on social identities. Finally, crip theorists bring to light how ableism functions in society in various ways (McRuer, 2006). Although these are reductive ways of presenting these theories, the significant takeaway is that scholars and educators engaging these frameworks in their understandings of student development theory must think critically about who these frameworks can engage. Therefore, identity interconnections can help challenge the belief that these theories are narrow in their application and instead encourage people to apply these ideas in expansive and responsible ways.

THE IMPORTANCE OF DEVELOPMENTAL CONSTRUCTS

As noted previously, the third wave of student development theory illustrates how researchers and educators can think beyond previous conceptualizations of development. Namely, though the first and second waves frequently showcased how development was represented in the form of statuses, stages, phases, or vectors, the third wave invites individuals to consider how enduring constructs related to development appear across domains and identities. For instance, in Abes et al.'s (2019) text, authors reimagined notions of resilience within college students, how agency manifests for individuals, and how context shapes the nature of development; this type of theorizing opens up the potential for identity interconnections to thrive.

When applying developmental constructs in the third wave, individuals should think critically about how systems of power influence a particular population and their development and may also be manifesting in the lives of others—by either serving as a point of oppression or leading to an experience of privilege. For example, in their chapter on reconceptualizing ways of knowing, Waterman and Bazemore-James (2019) applied indigenous knowledge systems (IKS) to identify how Western colonizer schools of thought constrain knowledge creation for Indigenous individuals. This contribution to the student development canon is imperative because the authors argued how people frequently think of knowing from a perspective that centers the individual and meritocratic systems. By instead emphasizing the centrality of relationships and culture, Waterman and Bazemore-James (2019) challenged existing understandings of cognitive development, which pushed the field's understanding of knowing broadly. Consequently, these ideas may encourage scholars and practitioners to consider how they have perpetuated Western thinking that is ingrained in settler colonialism. This reflection could then be used to investigate the context in which all students are situated. This critical interrogation of multiple ways of knowing does not negate the particular impact that settler colonialism has had on Indigenous knowing specifically, but it also challenges individuals to expansively understand and consider how dynamics around knowing are symptomatic of bigger schema of how power plays out. Thus, when developmental constructs are reimagined with the help of critical and poststructural frameworks, identity interconnections can be a central part of these examinations and applications.

NOTES ON STEWARDSHIP

Although there is a great deal of potential in applying identity interconnections within the realm of student development theory, it is imperative for individuals to practice stewardship when engaging this work. In naming the need for responsible stewardship, I echo the introduction of this text where A. Ashlee and Combs discuss compassionate caution.

In particular, I caution scholars and educators against producing messy or simplistic applications of identity interconnections, specifically when interrogating the role that power, privilege, and oppression play in shaping the lives of students. Specifically, in the case of intersectionality, scholars have worried about its misapplication and misappropriation by individuals who have applied the framework haphazardly and who have overlooked the theoretical integrity and true analytic potential. This critique exists both outside of higher education (Collins, 2015; Davis, 2008; May, 2015) and within the field (Harris & Patton, 2019; Núñez, 2014). Therefore, to combat the type of simplistic or misappropriated applications that have occurred to theories such as intersectionality, individuals should make it a point to understand the histories and genealogies that underscore these frameworks. By comprehending how these theories came to be and how populations have long engaged in this kind of analysis, scholars and educators may be less likely to misapply these frameworks in their research and practice within the context of student development.

Additionally, another aspect of responsible stewardship that people must consider is wondering what occurs when applying this third-wave perspective to privileged social identities. In fact, many individuals who hold largely privileged identities may worry about where they fit in regarding the third wave of student development. However, it is imperative to recognize that privilege across all identities must be interrogated, especially as it pertains to students' development. Some examples of this work have started to emerge in student development theory as researchers have begun applying critical perspectives like critical whiteness studies to understand how whiteness and White supremacy play a role in student development (Foste & Irwin, 2020). Critical and poststructural theories are not solely intended to theorize marginalization but must also be applied across populations to examine privilege as well, a point that K. Ashlee and Cash also take up in chapter 8 on identity interconnections between masculinity and whiteness. Ultimately, third-wave ways of thinking, knowing, being, and theorizing can reveal possibilities for those who hope to transgress contemporary structures.

IMPLICATIONS FOR STUDENT AFFAIRS
PRACTICE AND RESEARCH

In examining how identity interconnections may fit within conversations of the third wave of student development, several implications for student affairs practice and research emerge. To commence, one of the central questions that emerges when it comes to critical and poststructural frameworks is to whom should these theories be applied? For example, scholars have long debated who is an intersectional being (Nash, 2008), with theorists asserting that people have not actualized the potential of the framework since privileged identities have been under-scrutinized (Carasthasis, 2008). Similarly, in a previous work, my colleagues and I asserted that higher education scholars have not yet fully mobilized queer and trans theorizing as this body of scholarship has largely only been used to examine queer and trans people's experiences (Duran et al., 2020). What would it look like to employ these frameworks to generate knowledge beyond what is expected? In this way, identity interconnections could encourage individuals to conduct student development theory studies employing critical and poststructural frameworks across different populations, honoring ideas of interconnectivity (Keating, 2013) in the realm of development research. Noted previously, this application should not be done sloppily or without intention. When utilizing critical and poststructural theories that emerged from particular groups of individuals, it is imperative to practice responsible stewardship in the process by naming where frameworks originate and describing the implications of using said frameworks for various populations. And yet, taking lessons from identity interconnections may help open up a new generation of student development theory research that adds complexity to how the profession understands and facilitates development.

Beyond creating possibilities for future research, identity interconnections can also play a role in shaping practice. For instance, as illustrated in the previous vignette describing a situation in a student development theory classroom, graduate preparation faculty should consider how identity interconnections can be a useful framework when discussing developmental concepts. As the study of student development theory expands to allow room for constructs as opposed to theories themselves, identity interconnections can perhaps be a key avenue to frame discussions on development. Graduate preparation faculty members can encourage students to write about how developmental constructs may appear similarly across various identity populations and encourage students to think about how certain developmental tasks manifest for different groups. Activities and assignments should motivate students to think about the implications of engaging identity interconnections recognizing that this type of work must be done with intention. For instance, instructors can have students reflect on the genealogies of certain frameworks and theories before then challenging individuals to name the pros and cons of using these ideas with different groups of people. This implication is perhaps even more important as faculty members are likely to fall into patterns of how they teach student development theory that replicate what they have seen in the past (Harris, 2020). Identity interconnections may thus extend previous conceptualizations of student development, both in and out of the classroom.

Because a focus on student development is a central value of the field of student affairs (ACPA & NASPA, 2015), it is imperative that these discussions are not simply occurring in graduate preparation programs. Consequently, considering the relationships between identity interconnections and student development theory must also be introduced into the professional development opportunities offered to student affairs educators. For example, student affairs offices might consider developing workshops or community conversations focusing on the third wave of student development and the new advents occurring in this area of study. Central to these professional development experiences should be conversations about identity interconnections, discussing how ideas can be transferrable across various identity groups while also honoring the identities on which interconnections are based. In these spaces, the facilitator can ask the professionals which populations of students they have worked with in the past and the particular developmental tasks they have seen them encounter, especially when shaped by issues of power, privilege, and oppression. Then, the facilitator can encourage educators to articulate how these developmental tasks manifest across different identity groups and identify what this means for the ways they support students.

Related to the implication offered concerning professional development opportunities, student affairs educators should engage in ongoing reflection on how identity interconnections manifest within their interactions with students. In their model on how to translate theory to practice, Reason and Kimball (2012) emphasized that it is important to start with understanding formal theory (i.e., knowledge in the field) but that this must then be followed up with comprehending how one's institutional context shifts how they apply formal theory. To apply identity interconnections to this process, I imagine additional steps that can occur when using formal student development theory in one's practice. First, educators should ask themselves: upon which populations was this theory developed? Then, they should pose the question: what does it mean to apply this theory and the lessons from this formal knowledge to the specific student with whom I am working, especially if they do not identify with the population that I identified in response to the first question? These types of questions are imperative to mobilizing identity interconnections in ways that honor the origins of formal student development theory research (i.e., practicing responsible stewardship) while at the same time extending these ideas to the practitioner's particular contexts and the students with whom they are working within in their offices.

CONCLUDING THOUGHTS

The third wave of student development presents new perspectives on what form development can take in college environments. Importantly, by bringing to light constructs, as well as critical and poststructural frameworks, the third wave also invites in the potential for interweaving identity interconnections into how people can conceptualize development. However, the application of identity interconnections within college student development must be done with intention and by practicing responsible stewardship. It is only when scholars and educators think about how to be intentional stewards of these ideas that they can use identity interconnections to their full potential.

To return to the vignette introduced earlier in the chapter, two main questions were introduced by students: (a) "I'm straight, so I'm a bit unclear how these ideas apply to me. What does queer theory mean for students like me?" and (b) "I am a bit confused at the argument that was in the article about queer students with disabilities. What does it mean for people to come out twice? Does using the language/concept of coming out to describe disability identity serve to appropriate ideas from the queer community?" So how did the instructor respond in this situation? With the first student, the faculty member discussed the importance of thinking beyond queer identities when it comes to queer theory. In fact, the forces that regulate queer bodies and identities, such as heteronormativity, also shape the lives of straight individuals in some fashion. Thus, they encouraged the student to acknowledge the expansive ways that they can apply queer theory even though they may not initially see it as applying to their lives. As for the second student, the class engaged in a long conversation about how the construct of disclosure may apply across multiple populations even if the language of "coming out" was initially used to describe queer experiences. They articulated how to honor where the language emerged from while also using it as an analytic that captures the realities that other populations face. This brief classroom interaction highlights how identity interconnections may lend themselves to the study of student development theory—as long as it is done with purpose and with responsible stewardship.

REFERENCES

Abes, E. S. (2016). Situating paradigms in student development theory. In E. S. Abes
    (Ed.), *Critical perspectives on student development theory* (New Directions for Stu-
    dent Services, no. 154, pp. 9–16). Jossey-Bass. https://doi.org/10.1002/ss.20171

Abes, E. S., Jones, S. R., & Stewart, D-L. (Eds.). (2019). *Rethinking college student
    development using critical frameworks.* Stylus.

ACPA College Student Educators International & NASPA Student Affairs Admin-
    istrators in Higher Education. (2015). *Professional competency areas for student
    affairs educators.* ACPA & NASPA.

American Council on Education. (1994). The student personnel point of view
    (SPPV). In A. L. Rentz (Ed.), *Student affairs: A profession's heritage* (2nd ed.,
    pp. 108–123). University Press of America. (Original work published in 1937)

Brown, R. D. (1972). *Student development in tomorrow's higher education—a return
    to the academy.* American College Personnel Association.

Carastathis, A. (2008). The invisibility of privilege: A critique of intersectional mod-
    els of identity. *Les Ateliers De L'Éthique, 3*(2), 23–38. https://doi.org/10.7202/
    1044594ar

Chun, J. J., Lipsitz, G., & Shin, Y. (2013). Intersectionality as a social movement
    strategy: Asian immigrant woman advocates. *Signs: Journal of Women in Culture
    and Society, 38*(4), 785–810. https://doi.org/10.1086/669575

Collins, P. H. (2015). Intersectionality's definitional dilemmas. *Annual Review of
    Sociology, 41*(1), 1–20. https://doi.org/10.1146/annurev-soc-073014-112142

Crenshaw, K. (1989). Demarginalizing the intersection of race and sex: A Black fem-
    inist critique of antidiscrimination doctrine, feminist theory, and antiracist poli-
    tics. *University of Chicago Legal Forum, 8*(1), 139–167. https://chicagounbound
    .uchicago.edu/uclf/vol1989/iss1/8

Davis, K. (2008). Intersectionality as buzzword: A sociology of science perspective
    on what makes a feminist theory successful. *Feminist Theory, 9*(1), 67–85. https://
    doi.org/10.1177/1464700108086364

Delgado, R., & Stefancic, J. (2017). *Critical race theory: An introduction* (3rd ed.).
    NYU Press.

Denton, J. M. (2016). Critical and poststructural perspectives on sexual identity
    formation. In E. S. Abes (Ed.), *Critical perspectives on student development theory*
    (New Directions for Student Services, no. 154, pp. 57–69). Jossey-Bass. https://
    doi.org/10.1002/ss.20175

Dillon, F. R., Worthington, R. L., & Moradi, B. (2011). Sexual identity as a univer-
    sal process. In S. J. Schwartz, K. Luyckx, & V. L. Vignoles (Eds.), *Handbook of
    identity theory and research* (pp. 649–670). Springer.

Duran, A., Blockett, R., & Nicolazzo, Z. (2020). An interdisciplinary return to queer and trans* studies in higher education: Implications for research and practice. In M. B. Paulsen & L. W. Perna (Eds.), *Higher education: Handbook on theory and research* (Vol. 35, pp. 1–64). Springer.

Duran, A., & Jones, S. R. (2020). Complicating identity exploration: An intersectional grounded theory centering queer students of color at historically White institutions. *Journal of College Student Development, 61*(3), 281–298. https://doi.org/10.1353/csd.2020.0028

Foste, Z., & Irwin, L. (2020). Applying critical whiteness studies in college student development theory and research. *Journal of College Student Development, 61*(4), 439–455. https://doi.org/10.1353/csd.2020.0050

Hancock, A.-M. (2016). *Intersectionality: An intellectual history.* Oxford University Press.

Harris, J. C. (2020). "Socialized into the field": Exploring how higher education and student affairs faculty members are socialized to teach student development theory. *Journal of College Student Development, 61*(1), 1–17. https://doi.org/10.1353/csd.2020.0000

Harris, J. C., & Patton, L. D. (2019). Un/doing intersectionality through higher education research. *The Journal of Higher Education, 90*(3), 347–372. https://doi.org/10.1080/00221546.2018.1536936

Jones, S. R., & Abes, E. S. (2013). *Identity development of college students: Advancing frameworks for multiple dimensions of identity.* Wiley.

Jones, S. R., & Stewart, D-L. (2016). Evolution of student development theory. In E. S. Abes (Ed.), *Critical perspectives on student development theory* (New Directions for Student Services, no. 154, pp. 17–28). Jossey-Bass. https://doi.org/10.1002/ss.20172

Keating, A. (2013). *Transformation now! Toward a post-oppositional politics of change.* University of Illinois Press.

May, V. M. (2015). *Pursuing intersectionality, unsettling dominant imaginaries.* Routledge.

McRuer, R. (2006). *Crip theory: Cultural signs of queerness and disability.* New York University Press.

Miller, R. A., Wynn, R. D., & Webb, K. W. (2019). "This really interesting juggling act": How university students manage disability/queer identity disclosure and visibility. *Journal of Diversity in Higher Education, 12*(4), 307–318. https://doi.org/10.1037/dhe0000083

Moradi, B., & Grzanka, P. R. (2017). Using intersectionality responsibly: Toward critical epistemology, structural analysis, and social justice activism. *Journal of Counseling Psychology, 64*(5), 500–513. https://doi.org/10.1037/cou0000203

Nash, J. C. (2008). Re-thinking intersectionality. *Feminist Review*, *89*(1), 1–15. https://doi.org/10.1057/fr.2008.4

Núñez, A.-M. (2014). Employing multilevel intersectionality in educational research: Latino identities, contexts, and college access. *Educational Research*, *43*(2), 85–92. https://doi.org/10.3102/0013189X14522320

Okello, W. K. (2018). From self-authorship to self-definition: Remapping theoretical assumptions through Black feminism. *Journal of College Student Development*, *59*(5), 528–544. https://doi.org/10.1353/csd.2018.0051

Patton, L. D., Renn, K. A., Guido, F. M., & Quaye, S. J. (2016). *Student development in college: Theory, research, and practice* (3rd ed.). Jossey-Bass.

Perez, R. J. (2019). Paradigmatic perspectives and self-authorship: Implications for theory, research, and praxis. *Journal of College Student Development*, *60*(1), 70–84. https://doi.org/10.1353/csd.2019.0004

Reason, R. D., & Kimball, E. W. (2012). A new theory-to-practice model for student affairs: Integrating scholarship, context, and reflection. *Journal of Student Affairs Research and Practice*, *49*(4), 359–376. https://doi.org/10.1515/jsarp-2012-6436

Torres, V., Jones, S. R., & Renn, K. A. (2009). Identity development theories in student affairs: Origins, current status, and new approaches. *Journal of College Student Development*, *50*(6), 577–596. https://doi.org/10.1353/csd.0.0102

Torres, V., Jones, S. R., & Renn, K. A. (2019). Student affairs as a low-consensus field and the evolution of student development theory as foundational knowledge. *Journal of College Student Development*, *60*(6), 645–658. https://doi.org/10.1353/csd.2019.0060

Waterman, S. J., & Bazemore-James, C. (2019). It's more than us: Knowledge and knowing. In E. S. Abes, S. R. Jones, & D-L Stewart (Eds.), *Rethinking college student development using critical frameworks* (pp. 158–170). Stylus.

2

Interconnections Between Being Both

Exploring Intrapersonal Multiracial and Interfaith Identities

Kelli Campa

THIS CHAPTER EXAMINES THE relationship between being multiracial and interfaith and how interconnectivity (Keating, 2013) can affect a person's identity development. Multiracial identity is defined as someone who belongs to more than one racial or ethnic group (Renn, 2000, 2003, 2008). Interfaith identity is defined as someone who belongs to more than one religion or faith group (Miller, 2013). In this chapter, I reflect on my own identity development and how I learned that I was multiracial and interfaith by discovering language to name these identities in graduate school. I use narrative storytelling to discuss how having multiple salient social identities—which defy binary thinking—has impacted my identity development and how I have made meaning of these interconnecting identities (Keating, 2013). Lastly, I conclude with implications and recommendations for practice for the field of student affairs regarding these identity interconnections.

THEORETICAL FRAMEWORK

Keating's (2013) work on interconnectivity informs how I understand the identity interconnections in this chapter between my race and faith identities. I also draw from other theories (Miller, 2013; Renn, 2000, 2003, 2008) that have helped me understand the interconnections of race and faith, which I use alongside interconnectivity. Most of the literature I have read explores multiracial identity *or* interfaith identity. I have not engaged scholarship about what it means to be both multiracial *and* interfaith, which is why I explore the intrapersonal identity interconnections between multiraciality and interfaith identity in this chapter.

Keating (2013) writes about three lessons of interconnectivity to help inform identity interconnections. The first lesson, "making connections through difference, seeking commonalities" (Keating, 2013, p. 38) aligns with my experiences of being multiracial and interfaith and underscores that even those who share the identities of being multiracial or interfaith may experience those identities in different ways. For example, we may have in common the experience of feeling between two worlds (either in race or faith), but how we experience those salient social identities and even our own life experiences may be notably different. I cannot know what it is like to be multiracial with darker skin, as I am a light-skinned individual with White-passing privilege. I can, however, empathize and be open to hearing others' stories to gain a better understanding of their experiences. Similarly, being interfaith, holistically belong to one faith group as I practice two religions. My interfaith and multiracial identities are both liminal, meaning I experience an in-between space concerning my racial and religious identities. However, there are also differences across these experiences because race is a visible identity, whereas faith is often an invisible identity.

Keating writes in the first lesson of interconnectivity about being open-minded and learning from others. My experiences being both multiracial and interfaith affect my worldview and knowledge in that I am able to be more open-minded in talking to others because of my life experiences and identity development. I do not associate others' identities with overgeneralizations or stereotypes since, from my life experiences, I have felt the painful impact of being stereotyped. I can build common ground with those from differing race and faith-based groups because of my own positionality as someone who is multiracial and interfaith.

I understand that not everything fits in the binary of Black and White when it comes to identity development.

Although finding connection in ACPA's Multiracial Network helped me understand my multiracial identity, I am aware of the differences that exist within this group, and in fact the differences are one of the reasons why I have found community within the Multiracial Network. Network members don't fit in one racial box, yet even though our racial identities and experiences are different, we can still have a common experience of being multiracial. Although I don't have a lot of experience interacting with interfaith individuals, as I have only ever met one other person who identifies as interfaith, I believe the same concept applies. Whether the person is Jewish and Christian, like myself, or of two differing faiths, not being one religious identity would connect me to them.

The second lesson, radical interrelatedness, in Keating's (2013) theory is relevant to the overall components of this chapter and also to how we relate to one another in society more broadly. Positing our radical interconnectedness means being mindful of how we relate to each other, as we are all interconnected. Similarly, with my own identity, although race and faith can be very polarizing, having open and honest dialogues with others has been helpful in my understanding and helped bridge the gap when it comes to conversations of difference.

Fixating solely on differences across faith and race can be dichotomizing and often very divisive. Recognizing that what we do and think impacts others no matter how far or different they are from us puts into greater perspective why "interconnectivity and accountability are closely intertwined" (Keating, 2013, p. 49). We must be accountable in our thoughts and actions in order to grasp fully and understand from each other our commonalities and differences to "begin moving beyond binary thinking and dualistic self/other identities" (Keating, 2013, p. 52). With my narrative, I intend to move beyond binary thinking, to examine how that rigid thinking mechanism has affected me intrapersonally and the relationships I have with others broadly.

Listening to what others are saying with raw openness is the last lesson from Keating's (2013) theorizing of interconnectivity. This concept of speaking with vulnerability and being willing "to be altered by the words spoken" (p. 52) has been extremely helpful in my identity development. Although my identity experiences as a multiracial and interfaith person are different from my family, friends, and colleagues, having the ability to tell my story and acknowledge that these identities exist has been a validating process. Listening and being vulnerable have played a key part in my identity development as a multiracial and interfaith person. For example, I have found community with another person who identifies as interfaith and multiracial through shared and vulnerable storytelling and listening. This connection has also caused me to think about my own identity experiences in new and deeper ways.

NOT ENOUGH AND TOO MUCH

I identify as multiracial and interfaith. In order to understand my identity development, it is helpful to start with my family background. In 1986, my parents met at work and quickly fell in love. My father was originally from Guadalajara, Mexico, identifies as Hispanic, and practices Catholicism. My mother was born in Chicago, Illinois, has a family background identified as Eastern European (White), and practices Judaism. Both of my parents' families had married solely within their race and faith, so marrying outside of both of these contexts was challenging for my parents at the beginning of their relationship. My parents' siblings all had monofaith and monoracial children. Therefore, when I was born and raised in a multiracial and interfaith household, some challenging questions arose, such as would I be baptized, have a bat mitzvah, or have a quinceñera?

Being the first in one's family to do something can come with some barriers and challenges. Because my parents were the first in their families to marry outside of their race and faith, there was some initial skepticism from both sides of the family. Eventually, their relationship was accepted after they were married in 1989. I was born soon after. One of my first memories of realizing that I was different from my family came when I was about 7 years old, while playing with my cousins. An innocent conversation among three cousins remains a powerful memory for me even today. While playing at my abuelos' (grandparents) house, my cousins and I got to talking about how we all had different skin colors and how I, in particular, had a language barrier with my abuelos because I did not speak Spanish (my abuelos only spoke Spanish). I had the lightest skin color because I had one White parent, and my two cousins had two Hispanic parents, so they were different shades of tan and brown. One of my cousins made a comment that out of the three of us, I was White because I did not speak Spanish and had the lightest complexion.

Although not meant to cause racial dysphoria, this conversation was the beginning of my understanding that I was different from my family members. I was not monoracial like my cousins, but multiracial (Renn, 2000, 2003, 2008). However, at 7 years old, I did not have the language to formulate that as my identity and advocate for myself and my experience of not fitting in just one racial category. My liminal identity was further illustrated a few months later during the winter holiday season.

Growing up, I observed both Christian and Jewish holidays. Although interfaith was not a word I would learn until graduate school, it describes my family tradition and background related to the winter holiday season (Miller, 2013). Growing up in California in the 1990s, I had not met anyone who celebrated Christian and Jewish holidays or had another combination of two religions. I was the only person who practiced multiple religions in my classrooms. I distinctly remember a project from an art class that happened around the same time as the conversation with my cousins. My classmates and I were making wreaths for the upcoming winter holidays that our families could hang on the front door. Students were supposed to select either red and green or blue and white to decorate the wreath, depending on which holiday your family celebrated: Christmas or Hanukkah. I celebrated both and had to explain to my art instructor how I needed to have all four colors on my wreath since one of my parents was Christian, and the other was Jewish. I can still remember the other kids' bewildered reactions as my wreath was the most colorful and notably different from everyone else's. This was the first time I realized that my religious upbringing was very different from others.

Keating's (2013) first lesson about finding interconnectivity in making connections through difference was illustrated in these two stories. In both stories, I was able to feel a connection with my cousins and classmates even though we had such stark differences from one another in our race and faith. My understanding that race and faith could exist outside of a binary would be further explored through learning new vocabulary in graduate school. These two stories also complement each other as the first shows not feeling like I was enough, in my multiracial identity, and the second shows feeling like I was too much, in my interfaith identity. Illustrating the liminality of these identities starting with my family background is important in my analysis of identity interconnections between being interfaith and multiracial. In particular, the concept of "enoughness" (Ashlee & Quaye, 2020) is illustrated throughout my narrative (not feeling White enough given my multiracial identity, and not feeling Christian or Jewish enough given my multifaith identity) and continues to be something I am mindful of as I reflect upon my interconnected identities.

INTERCONNECTED OTHERING: EXCLUSIONARY QUESTIONS

As a multiracial and racially ambiguous individual, the phrase "What are you?" is something I have commonly heard myself and with others in the community. In California where I grew up, it was common to see other multiracial individuals. Before I started high school, my family moved to Houston, Texas, where being different was noticed and remarked upon. Hearing the phrase, "What are you?" was commonplace. As a way to cope, I made up a game where I would have people guess my racial and ethnic identity. It would take many attempts before people would actually guess the correct region. Often they would tire of the game and simply move on and change the subject. This felt dismissive, as if my actual identity didn't really matter even though they were the ones who had brought it up in the first place. It felt exhausting having to explain my identity repeatedly and even more exhausting to have to disclose my identity to those who felt entitled to know because I looked different from them.

This experience felt uncomfortable and othering to me. Othering means treating someone differently from you (Franco, 2015). I began to understand and conceptualize my racially ambiguous identity from this game as both White and monoracial People of Color viewed me as different. My experience with racial othering continued and eventually connected to feeling religiously othered once I started college. The exclusionary question changed from "What are you?" to "What are you doing here?"

I attended a Christian university for my undergraduate education. Starting in 2000, the U.S. Census allowed individuals to check more than one race and ethnicity box. However, my university did not have something similar for religion. Instead, students could only check one box for religion, so I checked Judaism. During my first week of college, I met my suitemates and we became fast friends by attending Welcome Week activities together. One of the activities that we attended was the annual Pastor Potluck. Being a Christian university, some pastors worked for the university and lived right off campus. They hosted between 50–100 students each year, where the only expectation was to bring a dish to share. You did not have to religiously identify a specific way to attend.

One of the first people I saw at the Pastor Potluck was a student I met earlier in the week at a comedy event. At the comedy event, I had shared with the student that I was Jewish and Christian when they asked about my religious identity, which was a common question at our Christian university. Not thinking anything of the previous conversation, when I saw the same student at the Pastor Potluck, I said hi. The student replied, "What are you doing here?" insinuating that they didn't think I should be at the Pastor Potluck because I identified as Jewish and Christian. Luckily, one of my suitemates saw the interaction and quickly changed the subject to make me feel less embarrassed and othered.

However, that quick question, "What are you doing here?" stuck with me. It brought up insecurities of othering similar to my racial identity and made me realize that my interfaith identity was not known or welcomed in similar ways to how my racial identity had been questioned and dismissed. In both instances, my peers couldn't fathom that I had multiple racial and religious identities. Instead, they perceived me as monoracial and monofaith, perhaps in part because these are the dominant ways of thinking about racial and religious identities. Keating's (2013) first lesson, making connections through difference, is utilized in this section to illustrate the commonality of being othered. Although the exclusionary question changed from "What are you?" questioning my personhood, to "What are you doing here?" questioning my belonging, a similar experience of othering is shown in different ways. These exclusionary questions about what others perceive make me different—either in my race or faith identity—have enabled me to build empathy and solidarity with those who also experience othering, bringing us closer. This common experience creates solidarity through our shared feelings and builds empathy through learning others' stories. The exclusionary questions around my racial and religious identities explored in this chapter are examples of identity interconnections. The bombardment of questioning my liminal identities throughout my life has left me feeling empathy for and craving solidarity with those who also hold liminal identities because I understand the feeling of otherness.

Keating's (2013) second lesson, of positing radical interrelatedness, was also explored in this narrative. Positing radical interrelatedness is being mindful of how we relate to each other (Keating, 2013). In my narrative I share how exclusionary questions around my identities made me feel othered. Recognizing how others' binary thinking made me feel enabled me to think more critically about times when I may have adhered to dichotomous perspectives in ways that harmed or hurt others. Remembering that what we do and think impacts others no matter how far or different they are from us (Keating, 2013) can inform our ability to be more accountable to the ways in which we may inadvertently (and unintentionally) perpetuate pain and oppression for others. This realization affected both my own identity development and my meaning-making process as an aspiring ally to others. I became more aware of interconnectivity (Keating, 2013) through feeling othered for my liminal racial and religious identities, which deepened my commitment to intentionally including those who may also hold expansive identities.

TOKENIZED, AND STILL NOT ENOUGH

After settling in to my first semester of undergraduate study, I received an email from the Multicultural Office asking me if I would help with a Hanukkah event. Hanukkah is a Jewish holiday celebrated around the winter holiday season, usually in December. It commemorates the Festival of Lights and is celebrated 8 nights by lighting a menorah. Since I grew up celebrating Hanukkah every year with my family, I quickly replied that I would be happy to help and attend the event. I did not know that I would be the only student helping with the event, which would be the start of being repeatedly tokenized as "the Jewish student" on campus. Soon after the Hanukkah event, I was asked to start a Hillel Club for the university. Hillel is a Jewish campus organization typically found on college and university campuses. As the Hillel club's founder, I quickly recruited other members and organized events and celebrations, including Sukkot, Hanukkah, and Passover. Unfortunately, many of my peers regarded me as solely Jewish, even though I identified as interfaith.

I learned of Birthright through being the Hillel Club president. Birthright is a program where individuals, typically college students between the ages of 18–26 years old, who identify as Jewish, are given a free trip to explore Israel and their Jewish heritage for 2 weeks. I was very interested in attending the trip to see Israel and explore my Jewish faith even more. On the application, I was impressed that you could pick more than one faith and was excited at the prospect of meeting other interfaith individuals on the trip. Sadly, my application was denied twice, citing that I was not eligible because I identified as interfaith. The juxtaposition of being tokenized as "the Jewish student" at my university, yet not being "Jewish enough" to qualify to participate in Birthright, created dissonance.

This experience was the first time that my religious identity was not seen as enough. It brought back memories related to my multiracial identity of not feeling Hispanic enough because I did not speak Spanish, or not feeling like I could claim being multiracial because of my light-skinned privilege. Keating's (2013) third lesson of listening with raw openness is illustrated in this story of tokenism. Deeply reflecting on my experience being tokenized as "the Jewish student" on campus, yet still deemed "not Jewish enough" by Birthright, caused me to critically consider the dangers of tokenization. Feelings of resentment and frustration from being forced into a rigid structure for both my racial and religious identities (again feeling like I was expected to choose which one race and religion to belong to) led me to recognize how tokenization in any form inhibits our ability to wholly accept ourselves and others.

These reflections surfaced questions of identity legitimacy, enabling me to draw identity interconnections between my experience of not feeling enough in my race to not feeling enough in my faith (Ashlee & Quaye, 2020). Drawing parallels between exploring and articulating my multiracial identity and interfaith identity led me to feel more confident and live authentically (Baxter Magolda, 2001). Years later I would eventually attend Birthright, continuing to check the interfaith box on my application, and revealing in my narrative that my mom passed away and I was seeking to gain some closure and become closer to my Jewish identity.

THE POWER OF LANGUAGE

In 2013, I attended graduate school for student affairs and higher education in the Midwest. One of my first classes was a multicultural class in higher education. This class explored different social identities each week. It was in this class where I first learned the term *multiracial*. Reading Renn's (2000, 2003, 2008) work finally gave language to what I felt about my racial and ethnic identity. I resonated with the theory's description of the decision to move among identities how identifying as multiracial may be related to one's social and physical spaces and dependent on if those spaces communicated a sense of belonging (Renn, 2000). I finally felt there was a word for how I felt about not fitting the typical cookie-cutter box related to my race and ethnicity. I had spent so much time in my life with White-passing privilege and not being believed about my multiracial and multiethnic identity. It was refreshing to learn that a word that described my identity existed, and that research is done on those who identify this way. I no longer felt alone within my racial or ethnic identity and was soon able to find ways in which my interfaith identity was acknowledged.

Through learning about and naming my multiracial identity of being multiracial, I found a similar language that described my interfaith identity, interfaith. During a student affairs conference I attended in 2014, I picked up the book *Being Both: Embracing Two Religions in One Interfaith Family* (Miller, 2013). The book focused on incorporating two religions into one family, something my family did when I was growing up. Having attended a Christian university, I had taken religious classes before, but I had never seen the word interfaith. In college, a religion professor used the word *monofaith* to describe those who identify with one religion, but I had never thought to extend that logic to devise *multifaith* as a term to describe those who observe multiple religions. Accessing language and learning about these identities enabled me to make identity interconnections between my multiracial and interfaith experiences. I saw parallels of how I felt between my multiracial and interfaith identities (e.g., noticing my difference from monoracial and monofaith hegemonic norms, feeling othered for my liminal positionalities, and being questioned about my racial and religious legitimacy for holding multiple identities within each category). As such, I was better able to understand my identity development through these intrapersonal identity interconnections and having a shared language from scholars to explore multiraciality and interfaith identities.

Equipped with language to describe what I always knew about my multiple liminal identities, it became easier to have dialogues about my multiracial identity and to share with others what my interfaith identity means to me. I quickly found other multiracial individuals and one interfaith individual where, when together with them, I could explore my identity development in ways I had not before. I was not questioned when I identified as multiracial and interfaith, but instead believed and embraced because of these identities. This coalition-building through understanding each other's shared experiences brought forth commonalities among our different identities and facilitated solidarity and empathy. The community and coalition-building that I found among multiracial individuals has enabled me to feel empowered to explore my interfaith identity (Keating, 2013).

Keating's (2013) first lesson, of making connections through differences and seeking commonalities, was illustrated in this section. I was able to better understand my interfaith identity through exploring my multiracial identity. Having the language to describe one identity was a catalyst for thinking expansively about the other identity. I was able to learn more and expand my worldview by being equipped with language related to multiracial research and interfaith identity. Feeling othered and tokenized because of aspects of my multiracial and interfaith identities helped me realize that my liminal identities could inform my worldview and enabled me to find community with others who also defied monoracial and monofaith labels and categories.

IMPLICATIONS FOR STUDENT AFFAIRS

In this chapter, I explored parallels between my multiracial and interfaith identities and how my identity development was deepened through drawing intrapersonal identity interconnections. Exploring identity interconnections can lead to expansive conversations for student affairs educators to have with students and colleagues on shared identity experiences across identity categories. Although identity development is nuanced and different across race and religion, examining commonalities across identity experiences such as navigating otherness or questions of legitimacy can help bridge and build coalitions among and between different groups (Keating, 2013). Exploring identity interconnections can create opportunities for dialogue and enhances student affairs educators' ability to connect with, listen to, and meet students where they are. Student affairs educators cannot do the critical work of helping students explore identity interconnections if we ourselves have not done the work; I hope sharing my narrative serves as an example of the ways in which identity interconnections can be formative to intrapersonal identity development.

In exploring identity interconnections between my race and faith, I have drawn parallels across oppression, tokenism, and feelings of enoughness between these salient identities. Sharing these connections with others has contributed to my sense of belonging within the ACPA Multiracial Network (MRN). Through programming in MRN, such as Mixed Messages (a virtual dialogue space for multiracial individuals and transracial adoptees to explore identity interconnections), I have engaged in raw listening that has enabled me to further explore my own identity development and meaning-making (Abes et al., 2007). Student affairs educators can facilitate programs like Mixed Messages to create collaborative spaces for social justice conversations that connect individuals across multiracial and interfaith identities. With the prevalent surge in universities' espoused commitment to diversity, equity, and inclusion, having conversations that connect intrapersonal identity development for faculty, staff, and students with topics about equity, opportunities for access, and privilege is critical in learning about these areas and in retaining faculty, staff, and students with minoritized (and liminal) salient identities.

In exploring the identity interconnections between being multiracial and interfaith, I found that these two identities have the potential to facilitate solidarity among seemingly distinct communities. Navigating otherness and notions of legitimacy may create opportunities for allyship and solidarity with others who have similar experiences of liminality. The identities I explored in this chapter do not have innate solidarity. In fact, faith and race can sometimes feel at war with each other. One way to facilitate solidarity across these groups would be to host identity-based conversations more frequently. Too often, solidarity across identity groups is relegated to one-time conversations, something we do at conferences or not at all. From my experience, identity interconnections can happen across diverse communities or intrapersonally. We do a disservice to ourselves—and our students—by not exploring the identity development and social justice possibilities of identity interconnections.

My experiences of interconnected othering and being tokenized—yet still not feeling enough—within my liminal identities demonstrate the power of intrapersonal identity interconnections. Existing beyond binaries in both race and religion creates a nuanced experience that few understand. Connecting feelings of exclusion and tokenization across my race and religion, coupled with the power of language, created opportunities to deepen my identity development. Furthermore, experiencing my race and faith outside the binary has ultimately led me to be a better ally for others who similarly hold identities that transcend rigid notions of identity. I have a better understanding of othering, tokenism, and oppression through my own identity experiences. I can empathize and listen with raw openness when having social justice conversations to become a better ally and show up for those who have been similarly marginalized and oppressed. My multiracial and interfaith identity development was catalyzed by my graduate school experience of gaining access to language to describe my liminal experiences, extend beyond binaries, and think outside the box. Having intentional spaces— whether in graduate preparation programs or professional associations—to explore identity interconnections has the potential to help others with liminal identity experiences to further understand their own identity development and create solidarity among these communities.

I suggest that, like with any identity-based work, student affairs educators come with an open mind and willingness to challenge their assumptions. I recommend that communities of practice be built for those who identify as interfaith, similar to multiracial communities that I have found within the student affairs field. These spaces for exploration could enhance the field through fostering intrapersonal identity interconnections. By encouraging reflection and action, informed by interconnectivity (Keating, 2013), I believe that intrapersonal identity interconnections can aid people who hold these two salient social identities—multiracial and interfaith identities—in identity development and social justice action. It is important for nonbinary groups to find each other and come together. A lot of identity development is done intrapersonally, through awareness and self-examination, and drawing connections between liminal identity experiences might enable individuals to make meaning of their experiences. Similar to how I identify outside the binary for race and faith, I am sure others identify outside the binary in two or more social identities. Naming this and putting intrapersonal identity interconnections into practice might help those who exist outside of binaries support each other in their differences as well as in their commonalities in their identity development. It should be noted that compassionate caution and the importance of examining differences between liminal identities is important because although there may be similar experiences across identities, distinct identities may develop and be perceived differently.

One concrete student affairs programming suggestion to support those who, like me, exist outside the binary in two or more social identities could host an event centering both/and identities. This would help those who are marginalized within two social identities connect with others to share language, stories, and hopefully develop empathy and solidarity. On campuses, student affairs educators could facilitate conversations about interconnected experiences of othering and tokenization across different identities to bring together diverse communities. All social identities (from race, faith, gender, sexual orientation, ability, social class, and more) could be invited to participate in an event like this. The conversation would explore commonalities and differences between how individuals navigate their interconnected experiences and could help facilitate identity interconnections across communities and further intrapersonal identity development. This type of program would provide students, faculty, and staff with the opportunity to support each other and name similarities and differences within and among each other. It would also allow others to explore intrapersonal identity interconnections outside of the two social identities, race and faith, that I discussed in this chapter.

I hope that others who do not fit neatly in one box can find power in the in-betweenness of their identity and permit themselves to explore intrapersonal identity interconnections as a way of deepening their identity development. This chapter explored how interconnected othering and tokenization across my multiracial and interfaith identities impacted me and created intrapersonal identity interconnections. My multiracial identity development helped inform and facilitate the exploration of my interfaith identity. Drawing intrapersonal identity interconnections between my liminal identities helped me facilitate a deeper understanding of my own identity development. My hope is that others who hold multiple liminal identities can explore for themselves their intrapersonal identity interconnections to further their identity development.

REFERENCES

Abes, E. S., Jones, S. R., & McEwen, M. K. (2007). Reconceptualizing the model of multiple dimensions of identity: The role of meaning-making capacity in the construction of multiple identities. *Journal of College Student Development, 48*(1), 1–22. https://doi.org/10.1353/csd.2007.0000

Ashlee, A. A., & Quaye, S. J. (2020). On being racially enough: A duoethnography across minoritized racial identities. *International Journal of Qualitative Studies in Education, 34*(3), 243–261. https://doi.org/10.1080/09518398.2020.1753256

Baxter Magolda, M. B. (2001). *Making their own way: Narratives for transforming higher education to promote self-development.* Stylus.

Franco, N. R. (2015). Body paradox: Multiracial students, minority status, and higher education. *Journal of Leadership, 12*(3), 51–61. http://digitalcommons.www.na-businesspress.com/JLAE/FrancoNR_Web12_3_.pdf

Keating, A. (2013). *Transformation now! Towards a post-oppositional politics of change.* University of Illinois Press.

Miller, S. K. (2013). *Being both: Embracing two religions in one interfaith family.* Beacon Press.

Renn, K. A. (2000). Patterns of situational identity among biracial and multiracial college students. *Review of Higher Education, 23*(4), 399–420. https://muse.jhu.edu/article/30110

Renn, K. A. (2003). Understanding the identities of mixed-race college students through a developmental ecology lens. *Journal of College Student Development, 44*(3), 383–403. https://doi.org/10.1353/csd.2003.0032

Renn, K. A. (2008). Research on biracial and multiracial identity development: Overview and synthesis. In K. A. Renn & P. Shang (Eds.), *Biracial and multiracial students* (New Directions for Student Services, no. 23, pp. 13–21). Jossey-Bass. https://doi.org/10.1002/ss.282

3

The Power of a Voice

An Accent as a Portal for Interconnectivity Across Borders and Disabilities

Hoa Bui

I CATEGORIZE ALL THE responses I receive from others when I open up about my background and identities into three main groups. The first group of responses is overwhelmingly supportive and empathetic because they share many of my identities. The second is laced with unintentional micro-aggressions and outright racism, to which I fight back with prepackaged oppositional defensiveness (Keating, 2013). The last and most confusing is a silent weightless ambivalence, where my listeners meekly respond with a vapid "Huh, interesting!" and let my stories dissipate into nothingness. Occasionally, I stumble upon a fourth group, where identity interconnections are drawn but not conflated. Rooted in interconnectivity (Keating, 2013) as a theoretical framework, identity interconnections turn an experience from typically exotic, strange, weird, funny, odd, or queer to legitimate and worthy. One of my most influential experiences with identity interconnections occurred in the crossroads of race, nationality, and ability. It opened the space for me to reimagine my long-established English as a second language (ESL) speaker activist identity and anchored my activist identity in the social justice movement beyond my most salient oppressed identities.

BACKGROUND: VOICES, LITERALLY AND SYMBOLICALLY

"Raise your voice." "Speak your truth to power." "Dialogue across differences." "Speak up." "Say their names!" Within various social justice circles, to claim and use one's authentic voice against injustices is as natural as breath is to one's vitality. Meanwhile, the nagging feeling that I—an ESL speaker—am an imposter speaking in somebody else's voice and accent always haunts me. This juxtaposition between the need for a voice and the lack of ownership over the English language has been central to my student affairs professional identity and ESL international activist identity. Even though I started learning English at the age of 7 and have been living most of my adult life in the United States, my Vietnamese accent—choppy, unnecessarily rhapsodic, and commonly absent of plural ending /s/ and /z/ sounds—stubbornly persists. My accent is "broken," neither sexy nor desirable like a French, Italian, or British (i.e., White) accent. I secretly curse my accent when a new colleague asks me, "Where are you really from?" Theorizing language and identity development (while distinguishing language from culture or nationality), Norton (2016) argues "that language is not only a linguistic system of words and sentences, but also a social practice in which identities and desires are negotiated in the context of complex and often unequal social relationship" (p. 476). I long assumed that the "unequal social relationship" was solely about the race or the foreign status of the speaker. As such, I lock my accent and its centrality to my being into my "already existing opinions, . . . cling[ing] with desperation and fierce determination" (Keating, 2013, p. 6). Thus, I surrender to the self-enclosed notion, the status quo, that whiteness is the gatekeeper of the English language.

I constructed an oppositional either/or absolutist consciousness: Only foreign ESL Speakers of Color know the weight of an "undesirable" accent, and vice versa, the accent problem exclusively belongs to foreign ESL Speakers of Color. Within the field of student affairs, leveraging the fact that there are relatively few student affairs Educators of Color who have an international background, I established an expertise in international education, and my accent shows up in my analysis to deliver a transnational critique to the global ubiquity of White supremacy. To establish a new connection that offers "an alternative to this status quo, with its essentializing dichotomous definition of reality" (Keating, 2013, p. 7) means to unroot my selfhood and professional worthiness. Placing myself in an "antagonistic" position against society (p. 3), I neither actively look for this opportunity nor believe that it is possible, just as an oblivious character in one of those sci-fi movies where multiple worlds exist yet remain invisible to each other (such as the Marvel multiverses) until someone stumbles upon a portal, a threshold of "multiple intersecting possibilities, opportunities, and challenges" (Keating, 2013, p. 10).

THE STORY THAT BROADENED MY HORIZON

Four years ago, Keenan, a graduate student colleague and the other main character of this story, and I entered professional staff training to prepare for the new academic year. This was my first year as a full-time resident life staff after graduating from my student affairs master's program, which Keenan was about to enter. Our predominantly White midsize public university is located in a rural, conservative area of the Midwest. With 60 full-time master's-level resident directors and graduate students, our department could be overwhelming, and people did not expect everyone to know each other well. Both Keenan and I were "the only" in the whole student affairs division. I was the only international Asian; Keenan, the only wheelchair user. Keenan has Spinal Muscular Atrophy II (SMA II), a visible genetic, physical disability causing weakening muscles along with other health complications. We had our own social justice causes that we advocated for, and so did everybody else. Keenan was a colleague who I knew by name and reputation. Even before starting the master's degree, he had established a reputation as a formidable advocate for disability rights during his interview for the program.

Day after day, 8 hours of icebreakers, team builders, small talks, and presentations, most details of our staff training blended together. However, I remember Keenan and an exchange we had about our accents. For Keenan and me, accent was the threshold identity interconnection between his experience as a person with a disability and mine as an international Asian ESL speaker. The training session was in a classroom with individual tables with wheels that could be moved around to maximize flexibility in the classroom setup. With flexibility comes (some) disorderliness. These rooms rarely have neat rows or large enough space for wheelchair maneuvering, so most of the time, Keenan sat at the front of the room near the entrance. The presenter had not arrived, and the staff started to settle in their seats. I happened to sit next to Keenan that day. I asked about Keenan's day and how the training had been. The room was bustling with chitchat about the cafeteria's predictable lunch menu, the unpredictable Midwest weather, or some-body's exciting weekend plan. As Keenan started answering, I realized that I could not hear him clearly. The background noise was loud. Keenan has a soft, high-pitch nasal voice that almost sounds like speaking with a sore throat. Not familiar with his voice, I intuitively started staring at his mouth and tried to pick up the key words to understand. Suddenly, my English insecurity gushed in. I did not want a new graduate student to think less of me and doubt my ability, a full-time professional staff, because my English listening seemed so poor that I could not keep up simple small talk.

However, coordinating my eyes and ears for comprehension while manag-ing my insecurity made me a bad listener. I couldn't stay focused on Keenan as my attention turned inward to myself. Meanwhile, knowing that I was an alumna of the graduate program, Keenan asked about the classes that I took in my first year, and I paused for a full 3 seconds after Keenan finished his question to begin my answer. This pause broke the natural flow of the conversation; I appeared distracted and uninterested. Haunted by stories and personal experience where native English speakers intentionally raised their voice or slowed down their speech while speaking to me or other ESL speak-ers, I am hypersensitive about the speed and clarity in my conversational repertoire. I am not slow, and I never want to be seen that way.

To pile on, I somehow could not pronounce the word "register" to say that "I register for a class because of the professor rather than the con-tent." "Register" has always been one of my problematic words, along with "perseverance" or "omnipotence." Instead of "REH-juh-str," the sound coming out of my mouth was more like "reh-TRIK-tr" or "rik-JUHST-tr"; each attempt sounded worse than the previous. I felt like a cook in a home kitchen, attempting a 15-minute one-pot dinner, then somehow 13 minutes in realizing that the sugar and salt were mislabeled. Keenan was still patiently listening and nodded along, not jumping in to say the word for me. Frustrated with myself, I ceased futilely repeating different iterations and carried on. "Ugh . . . you know, I, uh . . . took the class because of the professor rather than the content! Haha," I laughed nervously, "That word ['register'] is super hard for me!" Steering his wheelchair closer to my seat, Keenan smiled along sympathetically, "Oh, I get it, Hoa! English is annoying sometimes." I busted into laughter, "Yes! Haha, tell me about it!" The nervousness of the weird pause and the "register" debacle earlier slowly receded. Without missing a beat, Keenan nonchalantly shrugged, "Yeah, sometimes I struggled to say specific sounds too, because of my lung, you know? But I just tell people that I have an accent."

"What do you mean?" I asked, tilting my head toward Keenan's direction. I wanted to hear him clearly.

"Oh. I know that I sound different from people without this," Keenan responded, eyeing and pointing to his wheelchair, signaling his disability. "I just think, my voice isn't a disease! I am not sick. I have an accent, similar to uhm . . . say the Southern accent or yours."

Before I could respond, the presenter walked in. The session started and abruptly ended our conversation. I do not remember what I wanted to say to Keenan, but I ruminated on that moment for a long time the following days and even still years later. The whole conversation we had lasted less than 5 minutes, but it pointed me to a whole new universe—disability discourse—where one's accent influences their salient identity and their self-concept, yet positively.

ANALYSIS: IDENTITY CONNECTION AS
AN ANALYTICAL BINOCULAR

Had I the chance to discuss with Keenan, I would have shared my deep shame about my accent, not to discredit him but to invite him into my world. Even though our thoughts about the accent and its effects on our identity are opposite, we both recognized its power. Accent is the portal of interconnectivity—the identity interconnection—between our universes. To us, English competency is not just the ability to use complicated vocabulary to form sensible sentences with complex grammatical structures but also "the awareness of the right to speak" (Peirce, 1995, p. 18). Peirce powerfully explains this as "those who speak regard those who listen as worthy to listen and that those who listen regard those who speak as worthy to speak" (p. 18). This baseline for communication is often taken for granted by those with privileged identities, (mistakenly) viewed as universally available—given— to all people. With our visible and audible aspect of our marginalized identities, Keenan and I both have our own individual fight for the right to be heard and to speak. This baseline also serves as the prerequisite for Keating's (2013) third lesson for engaging interconnectivity, "listening with raw openness" (p. 38). Both of us took a risk to listen and create the opportunity for the accent "portal" to appear. When I struggled with my pronunciation, I could have given in to my struggle to hear him and diverted my attention to another topic or somebody else in the room to pass off the pressure to carry on the conversation. Yet, I stayed. In turn, Keenan did not judge me or my struggle over the long pause and the "register" pronunciation. He took a risk and opened up about his disability to create space for commonality with me. Keenan's insight on accent and its relationship to his disability compelled me to "re-examine and revise" my "most solid truths," my "most deeply held convictions" (p. 54).

To Keenan, the power of the accent construct lies in its disassociation with the medical model of disability. The medical model of disability frames the body as the central source of the difficulties and problems people with disabilities have in their daily lives. Consequently, the only option to improve the quality of life for people with disabilities is a cure for their illnesses (Wendell, 2000). The medical model disregards the noise level in the room and the inner turmoil and distraction running through my mind, which Keenan had neither awareness of nor ability to control, and places my inability to hear Keenan on him. A common alternative construct of disability is the social model: Disability is not intrinsic to the body but rather constructed by society, and society can remove structural barriers to increase access and life choices for people with disabilities (Waldschmidt, 2017; Wendell, 2000). My self-enclosed consciousness prevented me from even thinking beyond my own world, so I never realized that accent could belong to the social model. Accent is social due to its dependency on each person's geographical residency, first language, and economic background. Depending on the context, a person's accent becomes more obvious or subdued. For example, a White person with a Southern accent speaking English is just speaking English in Texas. However, if that person goes to Boston, they will notice that their accent becomes more prominent and they may have issues understanding Bostonian accents. Even though Keenan's accent is caused by his SMA II, my ability to listen and understand his voice is *not*. The medical model reduces a complex social interaction into a one-sided situation whereby the person with a disability carries all of the weight and gives zero expectation to the person without a disability. The medical model does not expect and give me the chance to do better by Keenan, and without pushing myself to be better, I could remain "blissfully" ignorant in my able-bodied privilege.

However, in saying that my accent has equal social standing with the Southern accent, Keenan, a White American man, does not seem to realize that accent is entangled in a racialized global context. Not all English accents and speakers carry equal power and authority. Researching ESL teachers and their perceptions of the ownership of English, Norton (1997) found a dangerous assumption about English that "only White people can be native speakers of English and that only native speakers know 'real' English" (p. 421).

More than 20 years later, this "native-speakerism," defined as "the belief that 'native-speaker' teachers represent a 'Western culture' from which springs the ideals both of the English language and of English language teaching methodology," is still prevalent (Holliday, 2006, p. 385). Lowe and Pinner (2016) found various pieces of evidence around the globe that native-speakerism resulted in negative student perceptions, low self-concept, and normalized discrimination of non-native speaker English teachers. Native-speakerism laces many slices of my linguistic life. The White English speaker with the Southern accent described previously is never under pressure to "cure" his accent regardless of where he is, Texas or Boston, whereas I am under this pressure, always and constantly. Every time an ESL speaker utters an English word, they are "not only exchanging information with target language speakers" but are "constantly organizing and reorganizing a sense of who they are and how they relate to the social world" (Norton, 1995, p. 17). Before talking to Keenan, I assumed that my accent combined with my Asian phenotypes further marked my perpetual foreigner identity, far beyond the realm of understanding for any White American. The identity interconnection with Keenan around accent pushed my self-enclosed understanding of my identity into new territory and challenged me to find the plane to hold both Keenan's understanding of his accent in the context of his disability and mine in the context of being a foreign ESL speaker. Just as Keating (2013) theorized, this "commonality" between me and Keenan offered a "pathway into relational investigations of difference" (p. 19).

While helpful, exploring the social model of disability and denouncing the medical model of disability do not fully cover the breadth of this identity interconnection between me and Keenan. Both of us recognize "accent" not only for its pragmatic value in our day-to-day participation in society but also, if not more so, for its symbolic value in our lives. Along with the medical model and the social model of disability, the cultural model of disability is used "to investigate the relations between symbolic (knowledge) systems, categorization and institutionalization processes, . . . and their consequences for persons with and without disabilities" (Waldschmidt, 2017, p. 24). The cultural model is the plane to reclaim labels of dominance and oppression such as "normal," "deviant," "fringe," and "legitimate." Keenan showed me that his disability is "not as a given entity of fact" but rather a result of collective "practices of (de)normalization" generated by "academic knowledge, mass media, and everyday discourses" (Waldschmidt, 2017, pp. 24–25). Therefore, Keenan can renegotiate his disability, and he did exactly that by intentionally choosing to name the peculiarity in his voice an accent.

How do I claim and negotiate my legitimate speaker title with this accent? My unresolvedness painfully demonstrates the need to pursue interconnectivity not only as a theoretical tool for analysis but also as a constant life and work practice. To enable interconnectivity in higher education, student affairs educators should start role modeling by asking our students different questions, sometimes removed from the time and space in question, and give them the opportunity to go deeper. I have been in too many diversity and inclusion training sessions for groups of 20-plus students where the presenter would encourage the students to share their stories and a student would respond, and then the presenter would call on a different student, thank both of them for sharing, and then make the connection between their stories *for* the students. As Paulo Freire (1970/2005) argued, this "banking" model of education trained the students to be "merely in the world, not with the world or with others; the individual is spectator, not re-creator" (p. 75). No wonder so many students and student affairs educators believe "that the way things are is the way they have been and the way they must be" (Keating, 2013, p. 35). Keating (2013) hints that these deeper questions should be pushing us to "a more ample 'awareness of the realities of the universe and our connections in it'" (p. 3). For example, I have never been satisfied with the simplified definition of appropriation, where somebody of one culture adopts, borrows, and benefits from aspects of a different culture. In various conversations I have had with students, while we recognize that a Native American Halloween costume is an obvious and offensive example, we get tripped up trying to draw the lines separating one culture from another and taking into account hundreds of years of colonization, war, and globalization. Specifically, is the famous Vietnamese "pho" simply a case of Vietnamese people taking credit for (i.e., appropriating) a Chinese- and French-inspired dish? The often-evoked distinction—appropriation versus appreciation—does not apply here (or does it?). Additionally, a dichotomous mentality still fuels this mindset. In what way do choice, capital, and power impact the culpability of cultural appropriation?

I would like to see smaller groups in a more contemplative setup where every story is honored, analyzed, and connected. Many institutions have been implementing intergroup dialogue, which is a structured space for "students from two different social identity groups" to engage in conversation in "a sustained and facilitated learning environment" (Nagda et al., 2009, p. 4), and this could be a starting point. However, intergroup dialogue does not seem to reach across categories of differences. For example, intergroup dialogue will bring people of different gender groups into conversation about gender, but to build identity interconnections across categories such as class, ability, and gender might be beyond the scope of intergroup dialogue. Additionally, student affairs graduate programs are not equipping incoming professionals with skills for interconnectivity. Courses on diversity, inclusion, and social justice often adopt a "compartmentalization" approach, which moves from one aspect of marginalization for a few class periods then onto the next one without asking students to create explicit interconnections.

IMPLICATIONS FOR STUDENT AFFAIRS PRACTICE

I stumbled upon a portal of interconnectivity that anchored both Keenan's and my worlds, but how could student affairs educators replicate this for themselves and their students? To "intentionally stumble" onto something is indeed an oxymoron! Thus, I urge student affairs educators to embrace the mindset of an angler rather than the straightforward "if X then Y" mindset of an IT programmer. Anglers do not know the exact location of any school of fish to cast their net, but they could make informed guesses based on the season, the time of day, the water current, and so on or attract fish to them by lures to maximize their success rate. Student affairs educators should focus their energy on creating semistructured environments so that students can converse and stumble upon their own interconnectivity portal. My programming experience showed me that if I would like to have a diverse group of attendees to facilitate deep interconnectivity, I should frame my events on a specific lived experience and then bring on the critical lens of social identity rather than the other way around. For example, one of my favorite signature events is an open mic night titled, "Oh My Hair!!!" where students share their hair journey. One's hair (or sometimes the lack thereof) can be a point of interconnectivity that cuts across race, class, gender, nationality, and so on. This chapter and the interconnectivity framework have inspired me to create another similar event that is called, "Ah My Accent!!!" Student affairs educators could use their own personal experiences with interconnectivity to guide student conversations. Just as in the story between me and Keenan, the most mundane conversation could result in the most life-changing interconnectivity moment. One could argue that interconnectivity is just a new label for something that has always been the currency, or bread and butter, of the student affairs world: We student affairs educators pride ourselves in engaging and educating students through the power of community and connections outside of the classroom. This understanding is only 50% complete.

Interconnectivity enables educators to articulate the idealistic purpose of our job. Not only do our events allow students to make the best of their current college experience, but our intentional work during these programs also fosters interconnectivity, underlaying the foundations for critically, socially, and historically informed compassion in young adults. The impact of moments of interconnectivity continues well beyond the end of the events, and even after graduation.

Although interconnectivity has powerful implications in the field of student affairs, interconnectivity should work in tandem with other strategies and initiatives rather than replace them. In particular, student affairs educators should consider a student's developmental positionality. Where is the student regarding their cognitive, intrapersonal, and interpersonal development? For example, a Black student who is developmentally in the immersion/emersion phase of their racial identity development might naturally want to be surrounded by symbols and people representing Black history, excellence, and solidarity (Tatum, 2003). A university should provide this student both the respite of an identity center and guided opportunities to cultivate interconnectivity with those with different yet similar salient identities (like the interconnectivity-informed programming I mentioned earlier, including the "Oh My Hair!!!" and "Ah My Accent!!!" open mic events). Interconnectivity is an important first step to build solidarity and cultivate creativity in addressing structural discrimination. For example, when female students in the STEM field express frustration when their professors do not value their voice in the classroom, through commonalities with others who are erased in different ways in difference spaces, they could benefit from knowing that erasure is a common, powerful tool of oppression, used not only on the basis of sex but also ability, class, and gender. My interaction with Keenan over the concept of accent taught me that I can step away from many assumptions I have about myself and the power that an accent has over me. That is inherently liberating.

Interconnectivity is both an educational goal and a part of the process to denounce injustices in higher education. Activist groups could employ interconnectivity as a powerful tactic to facilitate conversation on issues such as whether a university should cut funding for its women's studies program. The stake here is institutional erasure, and students and staff could use interconnectivity to flex their own muscle for empathy and imagination. Many stakeholders in a university have different visions for the institution, and as they discuss the issue at hand, interconnectivity could open doors and offer various solutions to this seemingly zero-sum game. Is there a point of commonality in every student's need for representation in the curriculum? The moment Keenan and I, both "onlys" in the department in the category of our salient identities, found a moment of interconnectivity, I felt a sense of belonging and affirmation. The process of answering the previous question might lead to unexpected destinations that could reframe the entire conversation. Maybe the conversation all along is not about money and retention but rather about which ways of knowing and whose existence are legitimate. With interconnectivity as a central framework, student affairs educators could be well equipped to lead a compassionate conversation centering the question, "How can the knowledge generated from the field of women's studies complicate, deepen, and/or enhance a computer science major student beyond profitability?"

I am pushing back against the tendency to view any new concept as "a silver bullet" for all our social ailments. Interconnectivity is a useful practice when students are aware of social injustices and want to look above the cloud of theories and critiques to find additional ways to cross differences and connect with others. As long as student affairs educators have this clarity, identity interconnections become a tool of empowerment. My story with Keenan was a memorable serendipitous portal of interconnectivity. I since learned to embrace the nonstructured downtime between meetings where small talk could turn into a seed of liberation. However, to rely solely on serendipity is not productive and might even be irresponsible for an educational institution. Student affairs educators should intentionally create a more interconnectivity-friendly space for students by helping students name tangible aspects central to their social identities (e.g., accent, hair, or wheelchair ramp). When a student articulates how this aspect affects their lived experience, the student affairs educator can ask other students to listen with raw openness and with compassionate caution find portals of interconnectivity. During these conversations, beside avoiding defensiveness and offensiveness, student affairs educators should specifically caution against cliché, rehearsed statements, vague generalization, or hollow agreements. These kinds of statements prevent students from listening deeply. When student affairs educators notice these statements, they can kindly ask students to rephrase using their own words and experiences.

Just as I felt seen, connected, and empowered when I learned that the accent has power in Keenan's universe, by intentionally finding and fostering identity interconnections, student affairs educators can bring in various populations of students that often feel left out of the higher education social justice discourses. These populations may include conservative students, international students, or students with invisible disabilities. Due to the apparent pervasiveness of "cancel culture" (where an individual is "cancelled," or boycotted, for seemingly problematic speech or action; Kurtzleben, 2021) and the emphasis on the need to be right and already "woke," these groups of students might feel underrepresented in social justice discourses. Identity interconnections could be a key for them to open new doors to claim their own voices and establish their own spaces for solidarity. This experience in turn might enable these students to consider how their feelings of marginalization are similar to (and distinctly different from) feelings of marginalization experienced by minoritized groups, creating opportunities for empathy. The more this reflection occurs, the less prevalent is the mentality that any particular -ism is somebody else's problem (e.g., sexism is women's problem), and the closer we are to a comprehensive approach to address all -isms.

REFERENCES

Freire, P. (2005). *Pedagogy of the oppressed* (M. B. Ramos, Trans., 30th anniversary ed.). Continuum. (Original work published 1970)

Holliday, A. (2006). Native-speakerism. *ELT Journal, 60*(4), 385–387. https://doi.org/10.1093/elt/ccl030

Keating, A. (2013). *Transformation now! Toward a post-oppositional politics of change.* University of Illinois Press.

Kurtzleben, D. (2021, February 10). *When Republicans attack "cancel culture," what does it mean?* NPR. https://www.npr.org/2021/02/10/965815679/is-cancel-culture-the-future-of-the-gop

Lowe, R. J., & Pinner, R. (2016). Finding the connections between native-speakerism and authenticity. *Applied Linguistic Review, 7*(1), 27–52. https://doi.org/10.1515/applirev-2016-0002

Nagda, B. A., Gurin, P., Sorensen, N., & Zúñiga, X. (2009). Evaluating intergroup dialogue: Engaging diversity for personal and social responsibility. *Diversity & Democracy, 12*(1), 4–6. https://www.researchgate.net/publication/312771261

Norton, B. (1997). Language, identity, and the ownership of English. *TESOL Quarterly, 31*(3), 409–429. https://doi.org/10.2307/3587831

Norton, B. (2016). Identity and language learning: Back to the future. *TESOL Quarterly, 50*(2), 475–479. https://doi.org/10.1002/tesq.293

Peirce, B. N. (1995). Social identity, investment, and language learning. *TESOL Quarterly, 29*(1), 9–31. https://doi.org/10.2307/3587803

Tatum, B. D. (2003). *Why are all the Black kids sitting together in the cafeteria? And other conversations about race*. Basic Books.

Waldschmidt, A. (2017). Disability goes cultural: The cultural model of disability as an analytical tool. In A. Waldschmidt, H. Berressem, & M. Ingwersen (Eds.), *Culture—theory—disability: Encounters between disability studies and cultural studies* (pp. 19–28). Transcript Verlag.

Wendell, S. (2010). The social construction of disability. In M. Adams, W. J. Blumenfeld, C. Castaneda, H. W. Hackman, M. L. Peters, & X. Zúñiga (Eds.), *Readings for diversity and social justice* (2nd ed., pp. 477–480). Routledge.

4

Impossible Bodies

Exploring Identity Interconnections Between Gender and Ability

Alandis A. Johnson

W HY DO WE THINK oppositionally? Binary logic—where someone is right and someone is wrong—is a commonplace way to deconstruct any argument; however, what happens when there is not a logical binary to dispute? What if the terms of the argument were instead fluid and flexible and capable of nuance? For example, gender and ability can be seen as infinite categories, in terms of the ways that people can embody aspects of these umbrella groups; however, some people still uphold that gender is a binary (men and women, cisgender or transgender) or view disability as a binary (temporarily able-bodied or disabled), which effectively erases people who do not identify with any/all of these labels. As Keating (2013) writes, "Oppositional politics and oppositional thinking have not enabled us to radically transform society" (p. 3). If that is the case, what can change others' thinking, bring diametrically opposed sides together, and ultimately have a more transformative result? The answer may lie in finding points of connection.

That is what I intend to do in this chapter: find points of connection between two disparate fields of cultural study—crip (or disability) theory and queer theory. By finding points of connection (while also acknowledging theoretical and experiential differences), there are ways that student affairs educators can use these theories to gain greater understanding and empathetic application with individuals they encounter. Gender and ability are both constructed identities, meaning that who is part of these groups has changed over time based on societal perceptions and attitudes. Queering (deconstructing within a fluid context) both domains shows how truly flexible and fluid they are within their embodied experience and temporality. Bodies are changeable, whether by one's own design (like with transgender people), or by birth or circumstance (because able bodies are not always so). Bodies can be altered. Time can alter bodies. Both sets of bodies—transgender and disabled—often get labeled as "impossible," as if unhuman; described as "grotesque" or "incomprehensible," as if to catastrophize the experience of existence within a body of either existence (trans or disabled).

In this chapter, I explore embodiment as another thread of poststructural discourse that weaves between these identities, looking specifically at identity interconnections between theories of gender and ability. I distill terminology from these fields by looking for points of connection and disconnection, and then apply it to my own experience as a nonbinary cancer survivor. Finally, I explore the possibilities surrounding the deconstruction and application of these theories and the potential implications that this process of drawing identity interconnections between theories of gender and ability may have for others, especially student affairs educators and members of minoritized gender and ability communities.

THEORIES ABOUT GENDER AND ABILITY

To begin, we first need to understand the poststructural discourses, or language imbued with power, surrounding ability and gender. Poststructuralism is a paradigm, or worldview, that looks specifically at power and how it has constructed aspects of society (Jones et al., 2014). Its main aim is deconstruction of these aspects of society in an effort to examine how power has impacted this group or concept (e.g., queer people, ability as a concept, imprisonment and/or the prison system). Identifying where power is placed and how power is used can assist in changing systems in the future, although poststructuralism makes no claims on how to go about transforming society or aspects therein. In this chapter, I use queer theory to deconstruct the language that is used to talk about trans and disabled bodies as "impossible." By understanding how scholars discuss overarching theory that deals with these expansive groups, I deconstruct terminology that is present in both theoretical bases—namely liminality, temporality, futurity, failure, and impossibility. I first discuss theories surrounding disability for both mind and body, as well as typical models for how disability scholars talk about impairment in all its forms. Then, I discuss queer theory. Finally, I explore these interconnections and what they imply for distilling a queer crip identity model to use as the foundation for deconstructing my own experience as a nonbinary cancer survivor.

Models About Disability

Many different models of disability are commonly used, and it is important to recognize which one is operating in any given sphere of influence, as these models guide the types of discourses that exist in specific contexts.

Mind and Body Distinctions Within Disability

Disability as a field is commonly broken into two subsidiary parts: impairments of the mind and impairments of the body (Kafer, 2013). It is important to recognize that each type affects individuals differently, as those with bodily impairments are often more visible than those with impairments to the mind. For example, someone in a wheelchair will likely have a very different experience with ableism than someone who is neurodivergent. Even still, both individuals still fit under this umbrella of disability. Additionally, context is important when talking about impairment. According to Kafer (2013), "People with impairments are disabled by their environments; or, to put it differently, impairments aren't disabling, social and architectural barriers are" (p. 7).

Individual Model of Disability

This model looks at what it would be like to live with a disability as it is commonly seen and understood. More concretely, inhabiting physical disability is used as an exercise to generate empathy and awareness for people living with disabilities. The experience of disability is not fully deconstructed as a complex identity that interacts with other factors, and thus essentializes the experience of having a disability of any kind (whether mind and/or bodily impairment). As Kafer (2013) writes, "There is no accounting for how a disabled person's response to impairment shifts over time or by context, or how the nature of one's impairment changes, or, especially, how one's experience of disability is affected by one's culture and environment" (p. 4). Thus, this model constructs disability as the same experience across individuals with very different impairments and ways of living in this world. It is incomplete and insufficient at describing the experience of living with a disability of any type because it is so specific to an individual person.

Medical Model of Disability

This model uses medical intervention to frame disabled bodies as deviant and defective. Kafer (2013) remarks that "The proper approach to disability is to 'treat' the condition and the person with the condition rather than 'treating' the social processes and policies that constrict disabled people's lives" (p. 5). It positions disability as an exclusively medical problem in need of intervention.

Curative Model of Disability

This model predicates that disabled bodies should be cured of their underlying impairment. Furthermore, people with impairments should *want* to be cured of their impairments. It fetishizes long life as the preferred future (Kafer, 2013).

Queer Theory

Queer theory is a field of poststructural inquiry aimed at deconstructing language, most commonly focused upon queer subjectivity (i.e., those with non-normative sexualities and genders; Jones et al., 2014). Queer theory has been applied in a variety of different ways and in many different fields. For example, queer theory has been used to analyze drag performances through theater and people through fields like English, rhetoric, sociology, psychology, or student affairs. It could even be applied to processes and systems in the science fields to understand them better. Queer does not necessarily mean lesbian/gay/bisexual/transgender/queer (LGBTQ+) in queer theory, although that is where it originated. While no commonly held definition of queer theory exists, some concepts that are widely discussed within queer theory will aid in this analysis, namely liminality, temporality, futurity, failure, precarity, and impossibility. Next, I explore what these concepts generally mean in an effort for readers to see these concepts in action in my narrative, which follows after the theoretical bases. While these descriptions are brief, I encourage readers to think about where some of these terms may or may not apply to their own experiences. Learning about language within these discourses has allowed me to understand how to talk about my identities more fully and with more nuance than I could have previously without access to these terms. Language has helped me to make sense of these terms and what they can actually mean in practice in my own life.

This is the power and potential of identity interconnections. By thinking expansively, drawing connections and interrogating differences, across constructed identities (in my narrative, gender and ability) I have come to more deeply understand language to describe my experience and the power undergirding those words.

Liminality refers to fluidity surrounding identity or other aspects of the self, whereby no one is solidly fixed, but rather, constantly becoming an identity (Jones & Abes, 2013). Temporality relates to time within a specific context, but it is imbued in the case of queer theory as something not fixed, but changeable and fluid (Halberstam, 2005). In other words, liminality refers to identity and temporality relates to time. Futurity refers to projections of the future, as well as possibilities therein (Edelman, 2004; Muñoz, 2009). Failure recognizes queer people as failures to societal expectations—specifically surrounding heteronormative ideals of raising children and creating a model nuclear family structure (Halberstam, 2011). Precarity refers to the state of queerness being persistently insecure and disenfranchised, compared to those with privilege. Finally, impossibility relates to perceptions of others as an identity that is "impossible," whether by design or by birth, which in turn forecloses opportunities and access. Living as a trans person is frequently compared to living an impossible identity with no hope for the future or a good life—a kind of dispossession of one's own life (Butler & Athanasiou, 2013).

TOWARD A QUEER CRIP THEORY

Many scholars have articulated connections between queer and crip theories within original texts (Clare, 2015; McRuer, 2006). In many ways, there is a tendency of both theoretical bases to utilize poststructuralism as a paradigmatic orientation to both these identity groups, which could explain why there seems to be a precedent for queer crip theory (and the interconnective properties of these theories) to exist. While these two theoretical fields are not the same, they frequently utilize language from the other theoretical base to articulate the experience or the similarity in that experience. For example, McRuer (2006) wrote on the concept of compulsory able-bodiedness, comparing the experience of feeling a sense of compulsion for heterosexuality and the nature of having an able body. This concept could also extend to compulsory able-mindedness to situate this term with neurodivergence.

Kafer (2013) has written extensively on the connections between queer and crip theories, and more specifically, temporality and futurity. Kafer (2013) sees these as one and the same—queer time *is* crip time; however, temporality is more expansive in the case of crip time because people actually experience notions of queer time in real life. This equates to a slowing down, a need for flexibility, and a need for more generous scheduling.

NARRATIVE: MY IMPOSSIBLE BODY

I have always had a hard time discussing my body—not because I was ashamed of it, but more so because it has never felt like something I could change or possess as strictly my own. I was diagnosed with non-Hodgkin's lymphoma in March 2016, and my body has never felt the same since then. Before my diagnosis, I had already been living an openly queer and trans life. I had a partner at the time who identified as a cisgender woman; I personally identified as nonbinary and queer. Life was good, for the most part. Then cancer happened, and my conceptions of time, my body, and most aspects of normalcy got thrown out of the window. As someone living with cancer in a body that was already "not normal" by most socialized norms, I felt that this experience of living with cancer would just be another thing to live with, to overcome, and eventually, to live without. What I did not understand is how it would expand my awareness, open up my perspective to how others saw me, and also change the way that I related to the world. It shifted my views on the importance of time and how I had previously perceived time as a stable construct. It changed the way I viewed my body. It fundamentally forced me to change how I related to others in every instance. My life is not the same as before, and as difficult as it might be to understand this fact, I can honestly say that I am glad that I had cancer. I am happy to be permanently disabled. I am grateful for my impossible body.

When I was in the hospital, more specifically in the intensive care unit (ICU), time was fuzzy. I blurred in and out of consciousness as I was administered doses of dilaudid (also known as hydromorphone hydrochloride) every 6 hours. For those who have never experienced pain management drugs, let me say that the experience is like nothing else. The experience is like being on a drug like heroin: euphoric at the start yet devastating as the effects of the drug begin to wear off. Your body craves it after being administered it enough times, which luckily, my body was able to combat. Yes, the pain from chest tubes and incisions hurt, and the immediate relief that I felt after another dose of dilaudid was potent and debilitating, while simultaneously, time became fuzzy and indistinguishable. I do not remember much from the days in the ICU, which is precisely what I want to call attention to: queer crip time, or this idea of temporality shifting. Some days, I counted the minutes and seconds till I could get my next dose of dilaudid. When I was administered a dose, time stood still. Likewise, the days and hours and minutes and seconds all seemed to blur together into an incoherent picture that I could not repaint, even if I tried. My mind and body were incapable of doing so. Looking back, if I had to recall these events, I am sure that most of them would be difficult and traumatic to face. I have others' recollections of this time—moments that they have shared with me, but my own recollections are limited because of dilaudid. Time was impossible for me to follow; it simultaneously felt so fast and so slow. Nothing felt normal. Time has never felt "normal" since then.

Cancer treatment graciously gave me permanent "chemo brain," or what some may call a permanent impairment to my mind. Chemo brain feels like constant confusion, and the experience is amplified when I am tired, stressed, or anxious. Some days, this impacts my speech. Other days, it impacts my level of attention that I can reasonably provide. Overall, I feel these impacts every day. During the beginning of my cancer treatment, I had been seeing a therapist who was a Black, cisgender, heterosexual, pregnant woman. When she would ask me about my experience, she, too, was experiencing similar effects from growing a child in her womb—the experience known to many as "pregnancy brain." When we talked, it was encouraging to know that others were experiencing similar phenomena—losing track of words, thoughts, interactions, and the like. It was a similarity, but key differences like the temporary nature of her "pregnancy brain" versus the permanence of my chemo brain stood in stark contrast. Not to mention, in most cultures, pregnancy is something that is celebrated, whereas cancer is never something to celebrate. Even still, it was heartening to have someone who could empathize with my experience to some degree.

Cancer forced me to get very clear about my future. At the start of my treatment, I did not disclose that I identify as nonbinary, and I made it a point to not correct medical staff, even though being misgendered hurt. Caregivers, doctors, and nurses all made assumptions about my gender identity. Likewise, not discussing my nonbinary gender was a consideration that I had to weigh as I was going through treatment, which forcibly dehumanized the experience for me and made it more about survival than an ability to be whole. I had to identify as a "woman" to ensure that I had access to treatment and doctors that could save my life. I did this to survive. Being trans is not something that all doctors recognize. With the severity of my cancer prognosis, I could not risk disclosing my gender identity for fear that doctors would refuse to treat me. I made concession after concession when it came to prioritizing good care from a medical team versus them knowing that I was trans. No one should have to make this choice to survive, yet I have had to do this so many times. I know how to "pass" as cisgender. When medical providers would misgender me, I knew that it was because I chose not to disclose my transness to them. When my oncologist asked me about my desire to have children, she assumed that I was a woman and, more so, that I wanted children. When I shared that I did not under any circumstances want children nor to cryogenically freeze my eggs, I believe this signified to her that I was already always queer. My body was failing me; my body was failing my future.

As I lost all my hair and any excess body weight, I did not recognize myself. The funny thing about cancer is that it made me even more visually androgynous than I was prior. People frequently stared and made comments about me under their breath. On one occasion, I went to the grocery store with my sister, and I forgot to wear a hat to hide my bald head. My sister commented, "If one more person stares at you, I'm going to slap them!" I replied, "I didn't even notice." Like I said before, my body has never felt like my own. It has never felt like a place that I understood in all its complexity, nor something I attributed much time or energy to constructing. Cancer amplified this dysphoria, and to this day, I still have some detachment from my body, its impulses, and its base desires.

ANALYSIS OF IDENTITY INTERCONNECTIONS WITHIN MY NARRATIVE

The experience of being both queer and disabled has been a gift unto itself. Identity interconnections are the practical application of interconnectivity (Keating, 2013) and serve as a vehicle to engage coalition building across and between identities. Additionally, identity interconnections create the opportunity to examine one's positionality and identities in relation to other individuals and larger systems of power by examining differences across experiences. It is simultaneously easy and difficult to articulate the multitudes of interconnections and disconnections that I see between these two identities, while also recognizing how these identities are constantly changing and informing one another. While I still see myself as nonbinary, I have come to accept that visually portraying my queerness and transness is a choice, and I am still valid no matter how I dress or perform that identity. Similarly, I do not look like a person living with a disability on the surface anymore. That aspect of my identity has become more personal, more internal, yet it is still incredibly important in my day-to-day life because of the impacts that it has left. My survivorship of this disease has lasting effects that the individual, medical, and curative models could not fully encapsulate (Kafer, 2013). My breathing will be labored; my brain works harder than ever before to form coherent thoughts, even though it fights the effects of chemotherapy; my body will continue to cringe in permanent nerve damage despite looking like I live with no pain on the exterior. The main difference is that I have grown to love my body, in all its imperfections, through a redefinition of failure (Halberstam, 2011). Failure does not mean that my body does not work correctly. Quite the contrary, in fact. My body has been incredibly resilient—fighting through things that others without disability could not imagine. The same is true to live as a trans person. Trans people do not choose this identity because it is trendy; they identify this way to create a livable, congruent life. Failure to live up to societal standards is not actual failure of an individual; it is more so a failure of systems (Edelman, 2004; Halberstam, 2005). There is no one, true way to be trans, nor is there one, true way to be dis/abled. We exist in our multitudes.

Exploring the concept of time through liminality agitates this idea of solidly "being" any identity and how time can change bodies, as well as our concept of them. The conception of my own body, as well as the experience of time shifting from fast to slow, illustrates this point of a queer, crip temporality (especially during the first few days when I was on heavy painkillers; Kafer, 2013). Time since then has seemed to slow down, and I have a more difficult time distinguishing its immediacy. I forget things often, including deadlines. Temporality in my current environment seems as it was during my whole treatment period—both so fast and so slow—but it tends to more slowness now that I have adjusted to my new normal within cancer survivorship. Within this present moment, I find myself hearing others from across the globe share that they are experiencing something similar in these times of COVID-19 quarantines. How strange it is to feel this immediacy, this precarity, and simultaneously, this slowness that comes with being stuck at home. Similarly, with so many new individuals falling sick with COVID-19, they too will have to face their newfound relationship with disability; by all accounts this coronavirus has left lasting impacts on the body, enough to warrant a "preexisting condition" in the eyes of medical professionals. It will be interesting going forward to see the impact that this virus leaves upon society—especially in relationship to disability.

I also noted that I felt a disconnection, or some might say a dispossession, with my body (Butler & Athanasiou, 2013). It seems strange to fight within your mind for a future that is not guaranteed. When I was faced with the harsh truth that I had a very aggressive form of cancer that was actively killing me, I had a choice: fight or die. To fight meant to deny my gender identity while receiving treatment for cancer. To die meant an end to every other possible future. Treatment was not guaranteed to work. Whatever the case, my body was not my own during this period of time. I am reminded by Butler and Athanasiou (2013) of so many other people who have been dispossessed of their humanity: "How do we fight for the right to be and to matter corporeally when our bodies are battlefields that are never simply our own—never entirely under our individual control?" (pp. 98–99). When faced with the expectations of others, societal pressure to conform to the norm, and an unending desire to live a life of congruence, I have never felt like my body was mine and mine alone. There were always unstated expectations that I live a life that lives on (whether through children or my works). This failure to live on was by choice, and it represents a failure that I actively chose (Edelman, 2004; Halberstam, 2005). This choice to fight or die is something that I still reference to this day. So many people think of their choices within a frame of complicity, but we do have choices in how we frame our futures—through possibility or otherwise. While my futurity in terms of a child is a failure of my own doing, that does not negate the necessity of divorcing futurity from child-rearing. Futures are possible for all people, and it would be in our best interests to define that future for our own selves, rather than having some compulsion to live according to standards that someone else sets for you.

IMPLICATIONS FOR STUDENT AFFAIRS PRACTICE

I have long since advocated for queer theory being an accessible and transformative theoretical framework for imagining new futures for people with marginalized identities (Johnson & Quaye, 2017). Likewise, using theoretical perspectives from disability studies has great potential for student affairs. Exploring queer theory, crip theory, and moving toward a queer crip theory can provide expansive possibilities for student affairs educators to think— and thus support students—postoppositionally. Generally, theory from various identity-based fields is written in a way that discourages individuals from outside fields from using them, due to specific terminology and commonly accepted ways of thinking. One of the goals for my writing is to make knowledge transferable and applicable to other fields (like higher education and student affairs). By distilling heady, inaccessible language from other fields into more understandable concepts with narrative examples to illustrate those terms, I intend to ensure that access to other fields and bodies of literature is a worthwhile practice for student affairs educators to adapt. Expanding one's own body of literature that they can use in their everyday life and within their own practice in working with students, staff, and administrators is important, and having language to understand another's or one's own experiences can help to push us forward, empathetically speaking. I share my experience to help others have a glimpse into my life—not for pity or sympathy—because I value the utility of my perspective of being both trans/queer and disabled. This is not to say that my perspective is the only one that should be considered, as that essentializes my experience to that of others who may identify as trans and disabled and thus advances a false monolithic narrative. However, I do recognize that there are not many people who write from this perspective of being both trans and disabled. Society needs more of these perspectives, not fewer.

Ethically speaking, both of these marginalized communities have terms and histories that are extremely violent. By speaking from my own experience, deconstructing these violent terms, and by applying these identity interconnections with compassionate caution, I reclaim some of that power (similar to how the LGBTQ+ community reclaimed the term *queer*). For example, I know that had I outed myself as trans to my oncologist today, she would be inclusive and would have treated me with compassion and civility by recognizing my nonbinary gender as valid. I only know this now because we have known each other for 4 years, and she knows me and my body more than most people on this planet—parents and partners included. By distinguishing how I am applying these terms as someone who is a member of these communities, but certainly not the only one who identifies as both queer and disabled, I am making responsible choices to demonstrate the value of being both trans and disabled, and how those interconnections are of a benefit to me, as opposed to a detriment. It has allowed me greater empathy toward others who are not like me, especially those that come from minoritized identities like in the case of my former therapist. Understanding queer theory in relation to my body has been empowering, and I hope to encourage others who feel that sense of disempowerment to reclaim the language and define/dismantle/deconstruct on their own terms. In many ways, this also combats notions of monolithic identities by sharing how individuals with complex interconnections make sense of and talk about themselves in expansive ways, versus being constricted by the limits of language. The way we use language matters, as language has power.

Finally, higher education and student affairs educators need to inform themselves more broadly on transgender populations and people with disabilities. From my time within the university system, I found it to be overtly discriminatory. I do not say this to shock others, but to tell the truth. Many people within higher education environments stigmatize individuals with disabilities and individuals who are transgender, whether subconsciously or consciously. The overt discrimination happens often through discourse (i.e., language imbued with power) to further marginalize people who fall outside of normative depictions of gender and ability. This language is coded in terms that impart "professionalism" or "ability to meet deadlines" or "performing work responsibilities" in a specific way. By having a more open, fluid model of working with professionals with these various identities, I know from experience that students and staff follow suit. Students need "lighthouses" to show them that a good life with a disability or as a trans person is possible. They need to see that possibility represented in leadership. Students need to be exposed to perspectives that are different from their own. Likewise, student affairs educators benefit from this expansion of their worldview, hopefully making the university climate a more accepting, equitable, and inclusive place—not just for them, but for all people regardless of identity. Using fluidity to complicate how we see ourselves and how we see others is a benefit in this same way; it necessarily complicates our internalized thoughts, feelings, and behaviors that we have about ourselves and others in relation to our own understandings. While it is impossible to fully understand every human and all the socialized messages that we have learned throughout our lifetimes, queering these beliefs can and is a good first start to better self-knowledge and awareness of others' interconnections of identity and the messiness of the human experience. Embrace the mess. I guarantee that readers' lives will be richer and more complex than they previously knew or understood.

REFERENCES

Abes, E. S. (2009). Theoretical borderlands: Using multiple theoretical perspectives to challenge inequitable power structures in student development theory. *The Journal of College Student Development, 50*(2), 141–156. https://doi.org/10.1353/csd.0.0059

Abes, E. S., Jones, S. R., & McEwen, M. K. (2007). Reconceptualizing the model of multiple dimensions of identity: The role of meaning-making capacity in the construction of multiple identities. *The Journal of College Student Development, 48*(1), 1–22. https://doi.org/10.1353/csd.2007.0000

Butler, J., & Athanasiou, A. (2013). *Dispossession: The performative is the political.* Polity Press.

Clare, E. (2015). *Exile and pride: Disability, queerness, and liberation* (2nd ed.). Duke University Press.

Edelman, L. (2004). *No future: Queer theory and the death drive.* Duke University Press.

Halberstam, J. (2005). *In a queer time and place: Transgender bodies, subcultural lives.* New York University Press.

Halberstam, J. (2011). *The queer art of failure.* Duke University Press.

Johnson, A., & Quaye, S. J. (2017). Queering Black racial identity development. *Journal of College Student Development, 58*(8), 1135–1148. https://doi.org/10.1353/csd.2017.0090

Jones, S. R., & Abes, E. S. (2013). *Identity development of college students: Advancing frameworks for multiple dimensions of identity.* Jossey-Bass.

Jones, S. R., Torres, V., & Arminio, J. (2014). *Negotiating the complexities of qualitative research in higher education: Fundamental elements and issues.* Routledge.

Kafer, A. (2013). *Feminist queer crip.* Indiana University Press.

Keating, A. (2013). *Transformation now! Toward a post-oppositional politics of change.* University of Illinois Press.

McRuer, R. (2006). *Crip theory: Cultural signs of queerness and disability.* New York University Press.

Muñoz, J. E. (2009). *Cruising utopia: The then and there of queer futurity.* New York University Press.

5

Engaging Identity Interconnections With Compassionate Caution to Inform Aspiring Allyship and Coalition Building Between Multiracial and Trans* Identities

Kamrie J. Risku

STUDENT AFFAIRS EDUCATORS OFTEN find themselves cultivating college students' personal growth through various functional areas. Identity development theories play a critical role in guiding student affairs scholars and educators in facilitating holistic student development. These theories help identify, describe, and explain college students' behavior as they discover who they are in relation to the world around them (Patton et al., 2016; Torres et al., 2009). Student affairs scholars and educators have built a body of research that grounds our work in evidence-based practice about students' development and experiences (Long, 2012). Student affairs scholars, educators, and professional associations assert effective practice requires a comprehensive understanding of applying theoretical knowledge (ACPA & NASPA, 2015).

Despite this robust knowledge of identity development theory, there are gaps in the literature that leave marginalized students underserved. For example, research illustrates Multiracial students and Trans* students can feel isolated, misunderstood, and under-supported by their peers, faculty, and student affairs educators (Carter, 2000; Johnston & Nadal, 2010; Museus et al., 2016; Nicolazzo, 2017; Patton et al., 2016; Tran & Johnston-Guerrero, 2016). These feelings can be attributed to experiences, such as Trans* students being misgendered in class or Multiracial students being challenged about their racial authenticity (Harris, 2016; Nicolazzo, 2017). This chapter explores how drawing identity interconnections can inform aspiring allyship and coalition building across and between Multiracial and Trans* communities.

Identity interconnections involve a complex process that takes time and commitment; however, they can be powerful tools to explore one's identity in connection to others. This chapter focuses on identity interconnections as a self-reflection tool to inform aspiring allyship and coalition building. I connect the chapter with the book's overall theme by focusing on identity interconnections as a self-reflection tool to explore misconceptions, commonalities, vulnerabilities, and areas for aspiring allyship and coalition building in my understanding of the interconnectivity (Keating, 2013) across and between Multiracial and Trans* identities. To provide context for the chapter, I begin with a review of Keating's (2013) theory of interconnectivity and theories of Multiracial and Trans* identity development. Then, I share my experience with identity interconnections, which informs implications for practice that continue to dismantle monoracism and transphobia through the intentional exploration of interconnectivity and aspiring allyship between and among Multiracial and Trans* people.

DEFINITION OF TERMS

There are many ways to describe Multiracial and Trans* experiences. To provide clarity, I define how I use Multiracial and Trans* throughout the chapter.

Multiracial

Multiracial refers to a person who identifies themselves as belonging to more than one monoracial group (Root, 1996). In this chapter, Multiracial is used synonymously with Biracial and Mixed Race (Root, 1996).

There are five monoracial categories recognized by the U.S. Census Bureau: American Indian or Alaska Native, Asian, Black or African American, Native Hawaiian or Other Pacific Islander, and white. The U.S. Census Bureau (2017) classifies Hispanic, Latinx, or Spanish backgrounds as ethnicities. Being of Hispanic, Latinx, or Spanish descent reflects similarities in language and culture but not necessarily race (Pérez Huber, 2010). Guided by the work of Lindsay Pérez Huber (2010), I have chosen to capitalize racially minoritized groups as a form of linguistic empowerment. I do not capitalize white to "reject the grammatical representation of power capitalization brings to the term 'white'" (Pérez Huber, 2010, p. 93).

Trans*

Understanding one's gender identity informs gender expression and refers to how a person communicates their gender identity to others through behavior, clothing, hairstyles, voice, or body characteristics (Nicolazzo, 2017; Patton et al., 2016). Trans* is a term used to describe people whose gender identity or expression does not conform to the biological sex they were assigned at birth (Human Rights Campaign, n.d.). The asterisk is used to "open up transgender or trans to a greater range of meanings" (Tompkins, 2014, p. 26). In this chapter, Trans* refers to people with gender identities other than cisgender (Patton et al., 2016).

Despite any scholar's attempt to capture the diversity of gender identity in a singular word, gender is a fluid and dynamic experience that cannot be entirely encapsulated by the language with which we describe it with (Nicolazzo, 2017). I use the term Trans* because the asterisk symbolizes the multiple meanings of this gender identity. However, Trans* does not negate the need for terms, such as nonbinary and gender nonconforming, that may better describe a person's experience and gender development. Student affairs scholars and educators should honor the choices and language of each individual.

LITERATURE REVIEW

This literature review begins with an overview of Keating's (2013) conceptualization of interconnectivity and how I use it throughout this chapter. I then briefly examine the bodies of research regarding Multiracial and Trans* identity development in college in order to contextualize my process of drawing identity interconnections between these communities. I conclude this section with summarizing two studies that model identity interconnections between Multiracial and Trans* higher education professionals.

Interconnectivity

The identity interconnections explored throughout this book are grounded in *interconnectivity*, which Keating (2013) describes as the meaning-making that occurs when people explore similarities and differences in their identity and experiences. The personalized approach is an insightful and transformative exploration of experiences that builds more profound empathy and coalition building among people (Keating, 2013). Additionally, compassionate caution of identity interconnections is an essential function of the practice. In the introduction, Ashlee and Combs define compassionate caution as "an empathetic application of identity interconnections, which involves a deliberate examination of both similarities and differences across identities and acknowledges how inherited systems of power inform individual experiences" (p. 8, this volume).

Racial Identity Development for Multiracial Students

Racial identity development is critical for all students, no matter their race (Renn, 2000). However, before the 1990s, Multiracial identity development theories were mostly deficit models (Renn, 2008). Student affairs scholars and educators often sorted Multiracial students' identity development into a monoracial identity development process (Renn, 2008). For example, a student who identifies as white and Filipino may have their experiences described through an Asian identity development model rather than a Multiracial identity development model. It was not until scholars and educators began focusing on individual identity groups that the increase of Multiracial identity development began (Renn, 2008). This literature is divided into three distinct bodies: psychological studies, foundational models, and ecological models (Renn, 2008). For this chapter's purposes, I briefly touch on psychological studies and foundational models but focus more on ecological models.

Psychological studies made up the early literature regarding the identity development of Multiracial people, with studies pointing to poor mental and physical health outcomes (Cross, 1987; Morten & Atkinson, 1983; Stonequist, 1937). This research asserted being Multiracial creates uncertainty, intense internal conflict, and isolation because Multiracial people straddle two racial identities (Stonequist, 1937). This framework was the predominant understanding of Multiracial identity development until the early 1990s when researchers began exploring if Multiracial people could have a healthy identity development process (Renn, 2008).

Poston (1990) and Root (1990) were some of the first scholars to challenge Stonequist (1937) and prove Multiracial identity development could be positive (Renn, 2008). Their research found multiple ways Multiracial people defined their identities, and one way was not better than another (Poston, 1990; Root, 1990). Additionally, they noted societal influences, such as monoracism, played a role in how Multiracial people self-identified (Poston, 1990; Root, 1990). Toward the end of the 1990s, researchers began to advance these theories by taking an ecological approach to Multiracial identity development (Renn, 2008).

Ecological models began exploring factors such as gender, social class, peer groups, cultural knowledge, age, and physical appearance as impacting Multiracial college students in different ways than monoracial students (Renn, 2000, 2004; Rockquemore & Brunsma, 2002; Root, 1998, 2003b; Wijeyesinghe, 2001, 2012). These models show Multiracial identity development is incredibly fluid and personal. Research has shown how Multiracial identity development is influenced by various factors and results in a nonlinear identity formation process (Renn, 2000; Rockquemore & Brunsma, 2002; Root, 1990, 2003a, 2003b). Unfortunately, for Multiracial people, this development is also marked by negativity from monoracial People of Color and white people. Renn (2000) wrote, "Given the importance in student development and racial identity development theory of having a group of like-others with whom to affiliate, the inability of most Multiracial students to find such a group is cause for concern" (p. 415). These racialized experiences hold negative implications for the identity development of Multiracial students.

Gender Identity Development for Trans* Students

Trans* identity has been explored throughout various disciplines (e.g., law, medicine, psychiatry), but a dearth of research exists on Trans* identity development in college, with most research focusing on comparisons between transgender and cisgender students (Mayhew et al., 2016; Nicolazzo, 2017). In the early 2000s, higher education scholars and educators used medical perspectives to guide the identity development of Trans* students

(Patton et al., 2016). Trans* student affairs scholars and educators resisted this approach because it implied the Trans* identity was developed out of mental illness (Patton et al., 2016). This pushback sparked scholars to start studying Trans* students from a nonmedical perspective (Carter, 2000; Patton et al., 2016; Wilchins, 2002).

Despite the limited research since then, existing literature does suggest college can be an important site for identity development and expression that perhaps could not previously exist in a students' life (Patton et al., 2016). Student affairs scholars and educators began developing social-cognitive approaches to gender identity development. These approaches provided a way to examine personal, environmental, and behavioral factors that interact in relation to a students' gender identity development (Patton et al., 2016). A benefit of the social-cognitive approach is that it does not focus on predicting the outcome of one's gender identity (cisgender, Trans*, nonbinary). Instead, it recognizes identity development should not take a blanket approach (Patton et al., 2016). As such, there is still a strong need for additional scholarship on Trans* identity development to understand how these students navigate their environments.

Multiracial and Trans* Identity Interconnections

The practice of identity interconnections is an opportunity to explore Multiracial and Trans* identities; it can also serve as a site for transformative coalition building between these communities. Examples of this type of coalition building between Multiracial and Trans* people have been published on two occasions (Harris & Nicolazzo, 2017; Ralston et al., 2017). I now review these publications to offer context for how I engage identity interconnections as a Multiracial person to inform my aspiring allyship for Trans* people.

The first example is Harris and Nicolazzo's (2017) autoethnographic analysis of their identities (Harris is Multiracial, and Nicolazzo is Trans*) and experiences as faculty members. Their work aimed to explore how *betwixt-and-between* identities navigate academic spaces. The phrase *betwixt-and-between* was first used by Turner (1969) to describe people who "elude or slip through the network of classifications that normally locate states and positions in cultural space" (p. 95). Harris and Nicolazzo (2017) use this term to describe how Multiracial and Trans* people "exist between socially constructed boundaries of race and gender" (p. 2).

For 13 months, Harris and Nicolazzo (2017) wrote 17 letters to one another, exploring the similarities and differences of their experiences as faculty. Their work highlights the interconnectedness of the inherited systems of power Multiracial and Trans* people face. For example, they explored "the limits of visibility" (p. 8) in which Harris (2017) shared how she was often hypervisible to her white colleagues when it came to discussing issues of race and racism. However, her colleagues, monoracial People of Color, left her feeling invisible by excluding her from conversations relevant to race and racism (Harris & Nicolazzo, 2017). Nicolazzo (2017) shared a similar narrative of feeling "*in* but not *of* hir mother culture" (p. 9). These experiences, and experiences like them, often relegate Multiracial and Trans* people as outsiders because they do not fit within dominant race and gender binaries (Harris & Nicolazzo, 2017).

Another example of identity interconnections and coalition building between Multiracial and Trans* people is the experiences of Ralston, Nicolazzo, and Harris (2017). They share counter-stories about the complexity of their identities (Ralston and Harris are multiracial, and Nicolazzo is Trans*) as higher education and student affairs educators and scholars who find themselves betwixt-and-between. In Ralston's counter-story, she discussed the challenges of trying to feel whole in her Multiracial identity (Cuban and white). Harris' counter-story focuses on her research on multiraciality and struggling with the questions, "Is the very act of researching multiraciality separatist? How might my endeavors to help build supports and foster community for multiracial peoples in higher education take away from monoracial communities of color?" (Ralston et al., 2017, p. 22). Finally, in Nicolazzo's counter-story, they grapple with how they might develop a curriculum that centers Trans* scholars without worrying about how cisgender or heterosexual people may feel.

Ralston et al.'s (2017) counter-stories highlighted how tiresome it is to constantly question one's identity. All three scholars struggled with their sense of belonging because they felt colleagues and students misunderstood them. They found that by sharing their counter-stories, they created opportunities to expand student affairs research and practice to include more interconnected opportunities for Multiracial and Trans* people (Ralston et al., 2017). They then used their experiences to draw parallels to students' experiences who also hold betwixt-and-between identities and offer implications for how faculty and staff can unlearn racial and gender binaries to better support students, faculty, and staff.

Although not explicitly named as identity interconnections, these articles offer poignant examples of the power and potential of identity interconnections between Multiracial and Trans* people. The scholars showed how letter writing, sharing counter-stories, and engaging in dialogue can evoke deep empathy, connectivity, and allyship, which are central components of interconnectivity (Keating, 2013). Lessons learned from these identity interconnections can serve as examples for creating meaningful and thought-provoking identity interconnections that lead to stronger allyship. I intend for this chapter to contribute to the literature that builds interconnectivity between the Multiracial and Trans* communities.

MY JOURNEY OF ASPIRING ALLYSHIP THROUGH EXPLORING MULTIRACIAL AND TRANS* IDENTITY INTERCONNECTIONS

Over the last few years, I have prioritized developing a better understanding of my racial identity. That journey started when I began applying to graduate programs. While I was writing my personal statement, I shared how important it would be for me to commit to being an educator who upheld students' dignity through a holistic development process unique to their lived experiences and identities. Racial identity development was significant because my Black-white Multiracial identity was a salient part of my identity development.

When graduate school started, it became much clearer that I could not be the educator I imagined without heavy lifting. I needed to (un)learn much of what I knew about myself and those around me. As I embarked on this self-discovery journey, it became clear how deeply misunderstood my Multiracial identity was by my colleagues, classmates, students, and myself. Multiraciality was often referred to as being *in between* two racial binaries. This language was often well intentioned, but I did not see myself as in between Black and white identities or experiences. In many ways, I could not relate to my white mom or Black dad's racialized experiences. I recognized that my experience was unique to me, not split between two realities.

(Un)learning what it means to be a Black-white Multiracial person continues to be a complicated process for me. I am continually working to define myself beyond the monoracial paradigm of race, which often leaves me feeling isolated from those around me. Although this is a lifelong process, through deep and critical reflection, I have come to see myself as a whole person, not separated by my parents' racial identities. This exploration has pushed me also to start considering the many ways other identities may similarly be defined in between false binaries.

An incredible moment in my learning was during one of my final graduate courses in which my professor challenged our class to think about identities structured around binaries. I listened to classmates share stories about (dis)ability, socioeconomic status, immigration status, and I shared about my experiences as a Multiracial person. One story that stuck with me was about the gender binary. Although the specifics are not mine to share, I will say that this moment was transformational for me. At the time, I did not know what identity interconnections were. However, now reflecting on the experience, I have the language to describe what occurred in that space.

When this conversation took place, I was struggling with making sense of my racial identity. I questioned whether identifying as Multiracial meant I was rejecting my Blackness. But when my classmates started to discuss gender binaries, I began to see clear connections that existed between those experiences and my own. Nonbinary peers struggled with the pressure of feeling like they needed to choose a gender and stick with it, similarly I struggled with my racial authenticity if I decided to identify as Multiracial. We both seemingly felt invisible, like nobody understood our identities, and hypervisible, as if everyone was constantly dissecting our identity, all at the same time. These connections motivated me to further explore gender identity development.

After that day in class, I knew that I needed to take it upon myself to learn more about the Trans* experience. I had not heard of the practice of identity interconnections when I began this journey, although much of what I did was just that. I engaged with the scholarly works of Trans* researchers and educators. I was fortunate to share meaningful conversations with Trans* people about their lived experiences. I spent a good deal of time watching documentaries, movies, and television shows that centered Trans* experiences. I also put action behind my words and donated to crowdfunding campaigns and organizations that supported Trans* people. But most importantly, I spent time in deep, individual reflection on the biases I held.

As a cisgender woman, I had not given much thought to my gender identity or expression; so, I thought it would be best to start my reflections with how I defined gender. I found it most helpful to keep a journal during this process that I could review later. In my journal, I posed questions to myself, like "How did I come to define gender?" and "How do I reinforce gender roles?" I tried to be as authentic in my answers as possible, which meant I had to be honest with myself about how I perpetuated oppression against Trans* people. This exercise proved to be emotionally and mentally draining as I was ashamed of the biases I held.

At most, I journaled every other week to give myself time to process and analyze my answers. I found that over time, I grew in my understanding of gender identity and expression. For example, I knew that biological sex was not always synonymous with gender identity and expression. However, this led me to reflect on how gender roles inform everything from the types of clothes we wear to the occupations we think we are qualified to hold. In my reflection, I drew parallels between the function of gender roles and how racial identity can also impact small decisions like the clothes we wear or big decisions like the jobs we seek out. I had never considered the similarity in experiences, but doing so allowed me to develop a more profound sense of empathy for the experiences of Trans* people.

During this journey, I transformed my understanding of gender identity and expression. I developed a deeper understanding of race and gender that allowed me to more easily reject gender binaries as absolutes and feel more confident in my fluid and dynamic racial identity. Most importantly, I learned how powerful it can be to connect my experiences to other's experiences, and this bolstered my aspiring allyship for the Trans* community. I see the practice of identity interconnections as an essential framework to grow my understanding of others' social identities and the challenges they may face. Sometimes, the work was taxing, and other times it was refreshing. However, I have always known that I want my student affairs practice to focus on liberation, affirmation, and holistic support, which required a great deal of personal growth.

ANALYSIS OF THE IDENTITY INTERCONNECTIONS

The previous narrative is a snapshot of what I hope will be a lifelong praxis; a cyclical process of reflection and action. I see identity interconnections as a framework to grow as an individual and in community with others. Identity interconnections have no definitive starting or stopping point because the meaning-making that occurs will always be informed by external factors like religious beliefs, racial identity, or socioeconomic status. By virtue of the cyclical nature of identity interconnections and the fluidity of Multiracial and Trans* identities, there are seemingly infinite similarities and differences between Multiracial and Trans* experiences. As a result of conversations, research, and reflection, I examined some of the differences between Multiracial and Trans* experiences to develop a deeper, more authentic allyship for the Trans* community (Keating, 2013). Additionally, by considering similarities across experiences, I built sites for interconnectivity between myself and Trans* colleagues and students (Keating, 2013). I will explore some of those comparisons in my analysis.

Differences

One of the most striking differences was how Multiracial and Trans* people navigated public space. There were many ways this difference revealed itself in my exploration, some of which I understood from historical and contemporary contexts. For example, as a Black-white Multiracial woman, I anecdotally understood the fear of being Black and in public places where people may put you in harm's way because of their biases. However, my lived experiences—no matter how uncomfortable—were not life-threatening. Most of the time, people are intrigued to discover my racial heritage. I have rarely been met with disgust or confusion. That is not the same reality for many Trans* people.

By November 2020, it was recorded that 37 Trans* people were victims of fatal violence in 2020 (Roberts, 2020). Roberts (2020) reported several factors that lead to this violence including "anti-transgender stigma that can lead to the denial of opportunities in society, such as employment discrimination and exclusion from health care, as well as to increased risk factors such as poverty and homelessness" (para. 4). While anti-Black violence is prevalent worldwide, my personal experiences with anti-Black violence are minimal. However, this violence is common for many Trans* people.

I found recognizing the differences in Multiracial and Trans* experiences informed my aspiring ally development. At the beginning of my journey, it was much easier to focus solely on similarities across Multiracial and Trans* identity experiences. Exploring differences was one of the more challenging parts of engaging identity interconnections. Doing so highlighted the biases and prejudices I held and forced me to confront how I came to know and believe these biases. But to be an effective ally, one must use their power and privilege to dismantle inherited systems of power. In fact, investigating differences—and holding myself accountable to my cisgender privilege—was essential to enacting identity interconnections with compassionate caution as an aspiring ally.

Similarities

I also identified many similarities between Multiracial and Trans* identity experiences. I found one of the most common themes was the oversimplification of Multiracial and Trans* identities. I found that both communities are often asked to describe how we identify within the binary of white and non-white or man and woman. And when a Multiracial person challenges the monoracial paradigm of race or a Trans* person challenges the gender binary, they are often regarded with confusion and rejection. These experiences can restrict Multiracial and Trans* people's ability to express ourselves fully.

Another striking similarity was feeling as though our identities were performative. As a Black-white Multiracial woman, I often omit my Multiracial identity and racially describe myself as Black. It is often easier to explain a monoracial Person of Color identity than have to explain how I do not see myself as half-Black and half-white. While there are differences in how disclosure manifests for Trans* people, it may similarly be easier to pass as cisgender than have to explain how gender is fluid and dynamic. This is yet another parallel in our experiences that can serve as a site of interconnectivity (Keating, 2013). Amid all the negative similarities was a shared recognition of how important it is to discover your whole self outside the restrictions of monoracism and transphobia.

I started this identity interconnections journey to learn more about Trans* students' experiences in college. Still, as time went on, my (un)learning was pushed further than I could have anticipated. Exploring the similarities and differences of identity interconnections created opportunities for empathy, connectivity, and aspiring allyship. It helped me better understand myself in relation to those around me, and ultimately, it highlighted how Multiracial and Trans* liberation is linked. I found identity interconnections to be a powerful tool for the liberation of marginalized identities and presented many implications for practice (Lorde, 1984).

IMPLICATIONS FOR STUDENT AFFAIRS EDUCATORS

The exploration of identity interconnections between Multiracial and Trans* people allowed for a deeper understanding of myself and others. While I previously held a deep empathy for others' marginalized identities, engaging identity interconnections pushed me to consider how my privilege is interconnected to others' oppression. The ethical imperative inherent in identity interconnections—to proceed with compassionate caution—spurred me to reflect on my own positionality and develop a more nuanced approach to my aspiring Trans* allyship. As a cisgender woman I cannot fully understand the experiences of Trans* people. Still, the exercise of engaging identity interconnections gave me a framework to consider, analyze, and understand differences and similarities between Trans* identity experiences and my experience as a Black Multiracial woman. Overall, the exercise offered three main implications for student affairs educators.

An essential element in student affairs work is reflection (ACPA & NASPA, 2015). Reflection allows educators space to unpack the meaning of their experiences, consider ways to enhance their leadership potential, and deepen their ethical development (ACPA & NASPA, 2015). Reflection is also a critical tool in understanding what one could be doing better as an educator (Reason & Kimball, 2012). It can be challenging to incorporate reflection into everyday work, but it is essential.

Research demonstrates the importance of educators reflecting on their role in social issues such as racism, sexism, and classism (ACPA & NASPA, 2015; Freire, 1972; Reason & Kimball, 2012). Reflection was one of the practices I used when engaging identity interconnections, and I believe it profoundly affected me. I used journal reflections to ask myself hard questions to dismantle the stereotypes and biases I held about the Trans* community. Student affairs educators can engage in reflection through activities such as journaling, conversations with colleagues, or reading. However, what is most important is taking those moments to pause and make sense of what one is learning.

Next, by critiquing and dismantling normative and essentialist perspectives of Multiracial and Trans* identity development, student affairs educators can develop policies, programs, initiatives, and curricula that more adequately affirm Multiracial and Trans* identities. For example, studies have demonstrated Multiracial and Trans* students can feel isolated on campus because they do not fit the binaries of race and gender deeply embedded into the collegiate environment (Johnston & Nadal, 2010; Literte, 2010; Nicolazzo, 2017). A potential solution to combat this isolation is developing sustainable, programmatic opportunities that bring Multiracial and Trans* students together to facilitate identity development and community through identity interconnections. These opportunities can be offered by developing collaborative programming between Multiracial and Trans* student organizations or facilitating intergroup dialogue courses that examine race and gender. Opportunities like this can bring together Multiracial and Trans* students and allow for empathy and interconnectivity across similarities and differences, informing aspiring allyship and coalition building.

Finally, identity interconnections offer student affairs educators a framework to engage in critical reflection about Multiracial and Trans* identities, theorize possibilities for liberation outside of socially constructed binaries, and then apply this knowledge to practice. Reflexive practice is a necessary part of effective student affairs work, and it allows educators to consider what is going well in their practice and areas for improvement (ACPA & NASPA, 2015; Reason & Kimball, 2012). By engaging in reflexive practices such as departmental or programmatic assessment, structured conversations with colleagues and students, or individual reflection, student affairs educators can begin to theorize how their work may better attend to the needs of Multiracial and Trans* students. Only then can educators put these practices into place by way of policy changes or programmatic offerings.

COMPASSIONATE CAUTION: CONSIDERATIONS WHEN ENGAGING IDENTITY INTERCONNECTIONS

Although I found engaging identity interconnections between Multiracial and Trans* identity experiences to be profoundly meaningful to my aspiring allyship, it is imperative that identity interconnections are undertaken with compassionate caution. Therefore, I offer three considerations for ethically and compassionately engaging identity interconnections: (a) identity interconnections are not absolutes; (b) identity interconnections are not mutually exclusive; and (c) identity interconnections should not stop at personal connections.

Identity interconnections offer student affairs educators a tool to create personalized approaches to understanding across differences. Considering the contextual nature of identity interconnections, they should not be treated as absolutes, and contextual influences should be considered and named when engaging identity interconnections (Abes et al., 2007; Jones & McEwen, 2000). Multiracial and Trans* people are multidimensional, and their histories and experiences directly impact how they understand and define their identities (Abes et al., 2007). Providing context and history of these identities and developing an environment where they are honored is critical in facilitating productive identity interconnections (Tran & Johnston-Guerrero, 2016).

Additionally, engaging identity interconnections should not be limited to assume the identities of focus are mutually exclusive, coming together as separate entities to build interconnectivity. Students who are both Multiracial and Trans* have experiences informed by layers of racist and gendered oppression that can influence their core sense of self (Abes et al., 2007; Crenshaw, 1989). Student affairs educators must recognize how these students' core sense of self is affected by layers of oppression when engaging identity interconnections.

Lastly, to engage identity interconnections with compassionate caution, the exploration of similarities and differences in experience should not stop at personal comparisons. Individuals must consider the impact of inherited systems of power on these comparisons (Keating, 2013). Student affairs educators should encourage students not to compare the Multiracial and Trans* experience but to consider the interlocking nature of racism and genderism (Tran & Johnston-Guerrero, 2016). Exploring how racism and transphobia are both produce binary thinking allows students to consider how identity is situated (and limited) in strict confines, whether by monoracism or a binary understanding of gender.

CONCLUSION

The mere existence of Multiracial and Trans* identities challenges the binaries of race and gender. These identities defy the simplistic and fixed notions of race and gender identity. And while this chapter cannot speak for all Multiracial and Trans* experiences, this work is significant because it offers an alternative narrative that dismantles and decenters normative and essentialist ways of thinking about race and gender. All people deserve affirming, authentic, and holistic identity development. Engaging identity interconnections offers a new way to think about the development of Multiracial and Trans* identities, and that is liberating.

REFERENCES

Abes, E. S., Jones, S. R., & McEwen, M. K. (2007). Reconceptualizing the model of multiple dimensions of identity: The role of meaning-making capacity in the construction of multiple identities. *Journal of College Student Development, 48*(1), 1–22. https://doi.org/10.1353/csd.2007.0000

ACPA College Student Educators International & NASPA Student Affairs Administrators in Higher Education. (2015). *Professional competency areas for student affairs educators.* Author.

Bell, L. A. (2016). Theoretical foundations for social justice education. In M. Adams & L. A. Bell (Eds.), *Teaching for diversity and social justice* (pp. 3–26). Routledge.

Carter, K. A. (2000). Transgenderism in college students: Issues of gender identity and its role on our campuses. In V. A. Wall & N. J. Evans (Eds.), *Toward acceptance: Sexual orientation issues on campus* (pp. 261–283). University Press of America.

Crenshaw, K. (1989). Demarginalizing the intersection of race and sex: A Black feminist critique of antidiscrimination doctrine, feminist theory, and antiracist politics. *University of Chicago Legal Forum, 8*(1), 139–167. https://chicagounbound.uchicago.edu/uclf/vol1989/iss1/8

Cross, W. E. (1987). A two-factor theory of Black identity: Implications for the study of identity development in minority children. In J. S. Phinney & M. J. Rotherham (Eds.), *Children's ethnic socialization: Pluralism and development* (pp. 117–133). SAGE.

Freire, P. (1972). *Pedagogy of the oppressed.* Herder and Herder.

Harris, J. C. (2016). Toward a critical multiracial theory in education. *International Journal of Qualitative Studies in Education, 29*(6), 795–813. https://doi.org/10.1080/09518398.2016.1162870

Harris, J. C., & Nicolazzo, Z. (2017). Navigating the academic borderlands as multiracial and trans* faculty members, *Critical Studies in Education, 61*(2), 229–244. http://dx.doi.org/10.1080/17508487.2017.1356340

Human Rights Campaign. (n.d.). *Understanding the transgender community.* https://www.hrc.org/resources/understanding-the-transgender-community

Johnston, M. P., & Nadal, K. L. (2010). Multiracial microaggressions: Exposing monoracism in everyday life and clinical practice. In D. W. Sue (Ed.), *Microaggressions and marginality: Manifestation, dynamics, and impact* (pp. 123–144). Wiley.

Jones, S. R., & McEwen, M. K. (2000). A conceptual model of multiple dimensions of identity. *Journal of College Student Development, 41*(4), 405–414. https://psycnet.apa.org/record/2000-00479-003

Keating, A. (2013). *Transformation now! Toward a post-oppositional politics of change.* University of Illinois Press.

Literte, P. E. (2010). Revising race: How biracial students are changing and challenging student services. *Journal of College Student Development, 51*(2), 115–134. https://doi.org/10.1353/csd.0.0122

Long, D. (2012). The foundations of student affairs: A guide to the profession. In L. J. Hinchliffe & M. A. Wong (Eds.), *Environments for student growth and development: Librarians and student affairs in collaboration* (pp. 1–39). Association of College & Research Libraries.

Lorde, A. (1984). *Sister outsider: Essays and speeches.* The Crossing Press.

Mayhew, M. J., Rockenbach, A. N., Bowman, N. A., Seifert, T. A., Wolniak, G. C., Pascarella, E. T., & Terenzini, P. T. (2016). *How college affects students: 21st century evidence that higher education works* (Vol. 3). Jossey-Bass.

Morten, G., & Atkinson, D. R. (1983). Minority identity development and preference for counselor race. *Journal of Negro Education, 52,* 156–161. https://doi.org/10.2307/2295032

Museus, S., Lambe Sarifiana, S., Yee, A., & Robinson, T. (2016). A qualitative analysis of multiracial students' experiences with prejudice and discrimination in college. *Journal of College Student Development, 57*(6), 680–697. https://doi.org/10.1353/csd.2016.0068

Nicolazzo, Z. (2017). *Trans* in college: Transgender students' strategies for navigating campus life and the institutional politics of inclusion.* Stylus.

Patton, L. D., Renn, K. A., Guido, F. M., & Quaye, S. J. (2016). *Student development in college theory, research, and practice* (3rd ed.). Jossey-Bass.

Poston, W. S. C. (1990). The biracial identity development model: A needed addition. *Journal of Counseling and Development, 69,* 152–155. https://doi.org/10.1002/j.1556-6676.1990.tb01477.x

Ralston, N. C., Nicolazzo, Z., & Harris, J. C. (2017). Betwixt-and-between: Counter-stories from the borderlands of higher education. *About Campus, 22*(4), 20–27. https://doi.org/10.1002/abc.21299

Reason, R. D., & Kimball, E. W. (2012). A new theory-to-practice model for student affairs: Integrating scholarship, context, and reflection. *Journal of Student Affairs Research and Practice, 49*(4), 359–376. https://doi.org/10.1515/jsarp-2012-6436

Renn, K. A. (2000). Patterns of situational identity among biracial and multiracial college students. *The Review of Higher Education, 23*(4), 399–420. https://doi.org/10.1353/rhe.2000.0019

Renn, K. A. (2008). Research on biracial and multiracial identity development: Overview and synthesis. In K. A. Renn & P. Shang (Eds.), *Biracial and multiracial students* (New Directions for Student Services, no. 123, pp. 13–21). Jossey-Bass. https://doi.org/10.1002/ss.282

Roberts, M. (2020, November 19). *Marking the deadliest year on record, HRC releases report on violence against transgender and gender non-conforming people.* https://www.hrc.org/press-releases/marking-the-deadliest-year-on-record-hrc-releases-report-on-violence-against-transgender-and-gender-non-conforming-people

Rockquemore, K. A., & Brunsma, D. L. (2002). Socially embedded identities: Theories, typologies, and processes of racial identity among Black/White biracials. *Sociological Quarterly, 43,* 335–356. https://doi.org/10.1111/j.1533-8525.2002.tb00052.x

Root, M. P. P. (1990). Resolving "other" status: Identity development of biracial individuals. *Women and Therapy, 9*, 185–205. https://doi.org/10.1300/J015v09n01_11

Root, M. P. P. (1998). Experiences and processes affecting racial identity development: Preliminary results from the biracial sibling project. *Cultural Diversity and Mental Health, 4*, 237–247. https://doi.org/10.1037/1099-9809.4.3.237

Root, M. P. P. (2003a). Multiracial families and children: Implications for educational research and practice. In J. A. Banks & C. A. M. Banks (Eds.), *Handbook of research on multicultural education* (2nd ed., pp. 110–124). Jossey-Bass.

Root, M. P. P. (2003b). Racial identity development and persons of mixed race heritage. In M. P. P. Root & M. Kelley (Eds.), *Multiracial child resource book: Living complex identities* (pp. 34–41). MAVIN Foundation.

Stonequist, E. V. (1937). *The marginal man: A study in personality and culture conflict.* Russell & Russell.

Tompkins, A. (2014). Asterisk. *TSQ: Transgender Studies Quarterly, 1*(1–2), 26–27. https://doi.org/10.1215/23289252-2399497

Torres, V., Jones, S. R., & Renn, K. A. (2009). Identity development theories in student affairs: Origins, current status, and new approaches. *Journal of College Student Development, 50*(6), 577–596. https://doi.org/10.1353/csd.0.0102

Tran, V. T., & Johnston-Guerrero, M. P. (2016). Is transracial the same as transgender? The utility and limitations of identity analogies in multicultural education. *Multicultural Perspectives, 18*(3), 134–139. https://doi.org/10.1080/15210960.2016.1186548

Turner, V. (1969). *The ritual process: Structure and anti-structure.* Cornell University Press.

U.S. Census Bureau. (2017, March 8). *Hispanic origin.* https://www.census.gov/topics/population/hispanic-origin/about.html

Wijeyesinghe, C. L. (2001). Racial identity in multiracial people: An alternative paradigm. In C. L. Wijeyesinghe & B. W. Jackson III (Eds.), *New perspectives on racial identity development: A theoretical and practical anthology* (pp. 129–152). New York University Press.

Wijeyesinghe, C. (2012). Integrating Multiracial identity theories and intersectional perspectives on social identity. In C. Wijeyesinghe & B. W. Jackson (Eds.), *New perspectives on racial identity development: Integrating emerging frameworks* (2nd ed., pp. 81–107). New York University Press.

Wilchins, R. (2002). Queerer bodies. In J. Nestle, C. Howell, & R. Wilchins (Eds.), *Genderqueer: Voices from beyond the sexual binary* (pp. 33–46). Alyson Books.

6

Using Identity Interconnections to Understand Disclosure

How Examining the Interrelated Experiences of Working-Class Students and Students With Disabilities Can Shape Student Support

Genia M. Bettencourt

AVERY AND SAM ARE two first-year college students at Research University (RU), a public flagship university in New England. While they each had clear resources and routines that helped them succeed in high school, transitioning to college has brought new barriers and challenges. Both Avery and Sam need help but are worried that seeking out assistance will mark them as different from other students and result in stigma. Why? Avery is a student with a disability; Sam comes from a working-class family. Though each has a unique experience, the identity interconnections between their two journeys provide insight into supporting students navigating disclosures of marginalized identities.

Higher education in the United States was established to serve a specific demographic of students—wealthy White men (Karabel, 2006; Thelin, 2019). The centuries since Harvard's founding have broadened participation through legislation such as the Servicemen's Readjustment Act of 1944 (the GI Bill), the Civil Rights Act of 1964, and the Americans With Disabilities Act (ADA) of 1990. However, at its core, higher education often maintains its historical foundations as a tool of social reproduction. For example, children with parents in the top percent of income distributions attend Ivy League institutions at rates 77 times higher than those from the lowest quartile (Chetty et al., 2017). On campus, many postsecondary institutions center middle- and upper-class experiences (Armstrong & Hamilton, 2013; Jack, 2019). While a growing number of students with disabilities have pursued higher education, the proportion of those who enroll and persist to degree completion is lower on average than students without disabilities (Mamisheishvili & Koch, 2011; Snyder et al., 2019). The result is that students with marginalized identities must often navigate to and through college campuses as sites of exclusion.

While some students are immediately otherized on campus, students with hidden marginalized identities may negotiate a process of sharing their experiences on campus, hereafter referred to as disclosure. I define disclosure as the act of "communicating or sharing one's identity with others" (Miller et al., 2019, p. 307). The disclosure process can serve as a mechanism to access resources and community, but also can invoke stigma and stereotypes. While there are inarguably other contexts in which students may disclose a hidden social identity—such as the coming out process for LGBTQ students—here I explore the connections between disability and social class. These identities share several commonalities. While not all students "pass" by appearing as a member of the dominant group, many students with invisible marginalized identities may appear to be able-bodied or middle-class. To access support, these individuals must disclose their marginalized identity, often risking stigma to access resources.

In this chapter, I explore identity interconnections of disclosure between working-class students and students with hidden disabilities. I discuss how classism and ableism serve as systems of power that necessitate and frame the disclosure process within higher education. Using the framework of interconnectivity (Keating, 2013), I provide narratives for the aforementioned Avery and Sam, two fictional students who serve as composites from the many students I have worked with, to illuminate the disclosure processes. Then, I examine how understanding these processes of disclosure as distinctive but connected can help student affairs educators, faculty, and administrators proactively support students in higher education.

UNPACKING CLASSISM AND ABLEISM AND
THEIR INTERCONNECTIONS

Like their peers, Avery and Sam spend the first weeks of college trying to make new friends, adjust to college-level courses, and effectively manage the unplanned time in their daily schedules. Yet, Avery and Sam navigate barriers that peers without disabilities or from middle- and upper-class backgrounds do not. It is impossible to examine Avery's or Sam's experiences without understanding how broader cultural and social systems shape higher education.

The need to disclose one's marginalized identity is rooted in the fact that inherited systems of power privilege and center dominant identities (e.g., White, cisgender, middle- and upper-class, able-bodied) while erasing or marking as "other" those with traditionally marginalized identities (e.g., People of Color, transgender, poor and working-class, people with disabilities). To contextualize social class and disability, we must understand how power shapes those identities through classism and ableism.

Classism has been described as "the institutional, cultural, and individual set of practices and beliefs that assign differential value to people according to their socioeconomic class" (Leondar-Wright & Yeskel, 2007, p. 314). Classism frames interpersonal interactions and results in prejudice and discrimination directed at poor and working-class individuals (Garrison & Liu, 2018; Lott, 2012). Yet, even as social class is hypervisible, it is also erased (Ardoin & martinez, 2019). Reflecting on her journey as a working-class student at Stanford University, hooks (2000) described this erasure, noting "the closest most folks can come to talking about class in this nation is to talk about money. . . . The evils of racism and, much later, sexism, were easier to identify and challenge than the evils of classism" (p. 5). Instead, the dominant expectation is that everyone is middle-class (Garrison & Liu, 2018). Moreover, social dynamics exist such that people with social class privilege rarely know individuals from poor or working-class backgrounds or have meaningful relationships across classes (Lott, 2002), helping to maintain social class silos.

A further complication of classism is that there is no universal way to categorize social class. Multiple criteria and categorizations exist, including first-generation, low-income, and working-class. Even within these categorizations, specific definitions and criteria vary and lead to different understandings (e.g., Nguyen & Nguyen, 2018; Toutkoushian et al., 2018). Sometimes it is beneficial to speak across these categorizations, which I do by using the phrase *students from marginalized social class backgrounds*. However, I primarily focus on working-class students, defined through parental education (i.e., parents or guardians have less than a 4-year degree) and occupation (i.e., primarily blue-collar jobs; Hurst, 2010; Stuber, 2011). Using working-class categorizations positions dialogues about social class within dynamics of power, labor, and autonomy (Freie, 2007; Stich & Freie, 2016), more aptly capturing relationships within a classist system.

Ableism is used to describe the "all-encompassing system of discrimination and exclusion of people who live with developmental, medical, neurological, physical, and psychological disabilities" (Castañeda et al., 2010, p. 457). Through ableism, disability is seen as disposable, invisible, and even subhuman, while able-bodiedness is the ideal or norm (Dolmage, 2017). In higher education, ableism centers the experiences of students without disabilities and shapes campus to cater to their experiences. Subsequently, students with disabilities face stigma through faculty perceptions, lack of appropriate advising, college stressors, and quality of support services (Bettencourt et al., 2018; Hong, 2015).

Like social class, the label of disability is broad and diverse. The Individuals Education Improvement Act (IDEA), first signed in 1975 and subsequently reissued, outlines the conditions for incorporating accessibilities and accommodations into higher education. The IDEA designates different categories of disability, such as orthopedic impairments, learning disabilities, autism, and intellectual disabilities. While diagnoses and accommodations are ingrained in K–12 education, in higher education students are expected to go through a new process to register with disability services. These systems are largely different in higher education than in K–12, limiting many students' ability to access accommodations because they do not know or have the resources to go through the accommodations process (Kimball et al., 2016).

The result is a spectrum of both disability and social class identities in which some forms of marginalized identities are more visible than others. In cases where students may appear not to have a disability or present as middle- or upper-class, they may engage in a phenomenon known as passing. In passing, members of marginalized groups perform as though they are members of privileged groups (Barratt, 2011). Ableism and classism reinforce the pressure to pass by rewarding individuals appearing to be privileged and enacting bias and barriers against individuals whom disclose. However, many resources in higher education are predicated not only on students disclosing individual identities related to disability or social class but on obtaining the necessary documentation to prove membership in these groups (e.g., a diagnosis, the Free Application for Federal Student Aid [FAFSA]).

Examining the disclosure process for both disability and social class simultaneously facilitates opportunities for deeper understanding in higher education using the framework of Keating's (2013) interconnectivity. Through examining interconnections, Keating advocates for "the creation of *transformational identity politics* that deeply acknowledge, yet simultaneously move through, existing social identity categories" (p. 19, emphasis in original). Interconnectivity encourages relational approaches that invite individuals to bridge their perspectives and create new alliances. In the context of disclosure concerning disability and social class, though both identities are complex and unique, understanding the shared commonalities can provide new opportunities for coalition building.

A TALE OF TWO STUDENTS

Around week 6, Avery and Sam each begin to feel overwhelmed at RU. The obstacles they have encountered are now jeopardizing their success in college. Both students look back at their transition into college to try to understand what happened.

Avery's First Semester

Avery was diagnosed with ADHD and anxiety in her junior year of high school after her teacher noticed that she had trouble focusing in class. Initially, Avery's parents dismissed the idea that she might have a disability. However, after Avery had an anxiety attack during her Scholastic Aptitude Test (SAT), her parents agreed to take her for an examination and explore different solutions.

With the help of her family, Avery redesigned and organized her bedroom to minimize distractions and clutter. Her small, rural high school was ideal for negotiating her ADHD individually. She had known many of her teachers most of her life, including two who had coached her soccer team in elementary school. As a whole, they were very supportive about giving her extensions or letting her work in the teacher's lounge independently when the class environment was too hectic.

At the beginning of college, Avery didn't realize that she needed to register with the Office of Disability Services to receive accommodations. By the time she learned this information, her assignments were due, and there was no time to set up meetings with the office. Avery thought about talking to her professors, but she was primarily in large courses with hundreds of students. She worried that if she asked for help, her instructors might think she wanted special treatment. Avery told herself that since she was able to manage until late in high school without a diagnosis, she would be able to figure out college. The week before an important exam, Avery began getting anxiety attacks every time she sat down to study. Now, she is scared that if she tells anyone, they will tell her that she is not capable or smart enough to be at RU.

Sam's First Semester

Sam is the first in his family to go to college. His mother is a cashier at a dry cleaner, and his father works as part of a landscaping crew. Sam did well in high school and always wanted to go to college to become a doctor. While applying to college, Sam largely used the internet to figure out what institutions might be good fits and offer him the best aid packages. Though proud of him, Sam's family was unfamiliar with the process of applying to college and could not help him with his search. He knew they were also nervous about the cost of college and apprehensive about taking out loan debt. Everyone was elated when Sam was admitted to RU with a large scholarship package.

A month before college started, the apartment where Sam's family stayed caught on fire, ruining his laptop and most of his clothing. Sam's financial savings from high school all went to replacing those items and buying supplies for college. Then, Sam's mom was laid off during his first week of college when her boss abruptly closed the business. Sam sent most of his financial aid refund back home and immediately applied for numerous jobs in the area.

Now, Sam works on- and off-campus, picking up additional hours where possible to send money home for his parents and three younger siblings. During high school, he was often able to do homework between classes or over lunch to free up more time for work. In college, Sam lacks the same free time, and the rigor of his courses makes it harder for him to finish assignments as quickly. He tries to study at night when he finishes work, but he is often so tired that he has trouble remembering anything he read. Sam can't ask his family for help. He already heard his roommate say something dismissive about students who receive financial aid, so he is reluctant to share his struggles or ask for help. When so many other students in his high school did not go to college at all because they had to work, Sam feels like he should not complain and just bear it.

IDENTITY INTERCONNECTIONS

Both Avery and Sam are navigating larger systems of power, privilege, and oppression that shape their experiences within higher education and create barriers. Though each experience has its own nuance, there are many parallels to their college transitions and what it is like to navigate a hidden marginalized identity at RU.

Across the two narratives, the identity interconnections highlight shared areas related to the process and experience of disclosure. By unpacking the two perspectives in tandem, we can better understand how higher education institutions create the need for disclosure, the challenges of the disclosure process, and how students navigate disclosure in order to inform subsequent support within student affairs.

Prior Coping Strategies May Not Suffice

Both Avery and Sam had coping strategies in high school that no longer work in their college environment. In high school, Avery built relationships with teachers and found ways to minimize distractions to succeed. In college, amid big lecture halls and new people, Avery cannot navigate in the same way. For Sam, unexpected changes to his family's financial and employment situations eliminated the tentative balance they established when he was in high school and amplified the new financial pressures of higher education. While he had been able to do his schoolwork in high school with less dedicated time, the competing workloads between his academics and employment are now too much. As a result, his academics are suffering.

Higher education often serves as a new context for students that impacts how they experience different areas of identity. The context of RU has created new academic expectations, relationships, and barriers to navigate. As such, Avery and Sam are experiencing disability and social class in new ways that bring their marginalized identities to the forefront.

Support Is Predicated on Disclosure

In primary and secondary school, resources are often coordinated by schools without the student actively seeking them. Some schools and districts offer free lunch to all students in high-poverty areas without the need for applications through Community Eligibility Provision (CEP). Schools, in consultation with parents, put together Individualized Education Plans (IEPs) for children with disabilities to outline accommodations. However, in higher education students are expected to be proactive in seeking out resources and to disclose their identity to do so. Students must register with their disability services offices to get accommodations for disabilities. To acquire financial aid, individuals fill out the FAFSA. The disclosure process was rightfully described by Carrol-Miranda (2017) as a hassle as students are required to navigate bureaucracy and policies to get their needs met.

To add to the complication, neither process of disclosure can be completed only one time. Students with disabilities must navigate the accommodations process for each class in which they enroll. To qualify for federal grants and loans, students have to submit a FAFSA every year. Moreover, students with these marginalized identities often encounter additional barriers daily, such as a building with no elevator to access higher floors or an unpaid internship that is crucial for one's degree program. Amid the dynamic nature of higher education, students constantly navigate between the costs and benefits of disclosure.

Stigma Shapes if and How Students Disclose

Systems of ableism and classism place deficit labels on students with marginalized identities, making disclosure processes laden in stigma (Hong, 2015; Hurst, 2010). In both cases, marginalized identities are often seen as individual faults. Poor and working-class individuals are blamed for their social class, which is falsely attributed to individual failings (e.g., poor work ethic, frivolous spending) rather than systems of capitalism that structure uneven wealth distribution and inequality (Barratt, 2011; Piketty, 2014). In addition, working-class students may be labeled as ignorant or racist (Hurst, 2010), which may cause students to be further hesitant to disclose their working-class background. For students with disabilities, fear of being seen as taking advantage of the system and abusing accommodations can make students reluctant to disclose (Markoulakis & Kirsh, 2013). Students may choose to disclose their disability with trusted individuals only when necessary (Miller et al., 2017), usually to advance specific goals such as accessing specific resources or accommodations.

Indeed, success for both students with disabilities and working-class students is often seen as distancing themselves from their marginalized identities. The medical model of disability focuses on treatment for disability intending to cure an illness (Shakespeare, 2012). Social mobility is seen as the goal of higher education for working-class students, where graduation signifies entering the middle- or upper-class and leaving their working-class backgrounds behind (Hurst, 2010). Both of these logics emphasize assimilation as the goal of higher education. In both cases, disclosure is at odds with the pressure to assimilate and create distance from marginalized identities.

Disclosure Processes Are Similar and Unique

While there are many comparable contours of the disclosure experience, there is one key difference. Working-class students are often navigating between a home community that is also working-class and the middle- or upper-class culture of higher education (Hurst, 2010; Jack, 2019). To traverse between these environments, working-class students use strategies such as code-switching (Elkins & Hanke, 2018). In contrast, students with disabilities may or may not have family members with disabilities. Thus, students with disabilities may be navigating a dual disclosure process at home and in college. Understanding this nuance may foster empathy in thinking about the different contexts and needs within which disclosure may occur.

Across these points, identity interconnections can help provide insight and empathy into students' social class and disability experiences. By understanding the commonalities and differences of the disclosure process, student affairs educators can be better positioned to support students with disabilities and from working-class backgrounds. Moreover, the idea of disclosure may provide opportunities to lower financial and ability barriers for all students, meeting the needs of many individuals who may be affected by ableism and classism but not fall into marginalized categorizations (e.g., middle-class students navigating high financial burdens; students who benefit from alternative ways to gather and express information, like auditory). The following section provides specific recommendations to provide proactive support.

IMPLICATIONS FOR STUDENT AFFAIRS PRACTICE

Avery and Sam live in the same residence hall at RU, led by a resident director named Martha. Unbeknownst to each other, each student discloses to Martha. Avery has a panic attack in the common restroom after class one day that results in her resident advisor referring her to Martha; Sam sets up an appointment to ask about the possibility of a refund for housing costs if he withdraws mid-semester. Though neither situation is the same, the similarities of the two students help Martha to better understand the factors that necessitate disclosure. This deeper insight helps her to act in support of Avery and Sam. She also gains greater empathy and knowledge to support other students with disabilities, working-class students, and students with hidden marginalized identities who might be encountering the disclosure process. Thus, the identity interconnections between disclosure of disability and social class provide important implications for student affairs practice.

Too often in higher education, the onus for success for marginalized student populations lies on students themselves. While resources exist, such as financial aid and disability resources offices, students need to seek them out for assistance. Moreover, a student with multiple marginalized identities (e.g., a working-class student with disabilities) may need to disclose repeatedly on campus to access different services and may not have a space to discuss intersectional concerns (e.g., barriers created by the high cost of accessibility equipment; limitations on employment opportunities). The need to continually navigate distinctive spaces on campus to obtain support can be a lot to navigate for undergraduate students (Harper et al., 2011). The mental energy needed to navigate this process has been referred to as a cognitive load, which can divert students' time away from academics (Fox et al., 2007; Kezar et al., 2020).

Instead, student affairs educators can and should strive to create proactive, inclusive opportunities that do not rely solely on disclosure of identity. McNair et al. (2016) emphasize proactivity as the key to ensuring that institutions are student ready to support the diverse needs of individuals rather than expecting students to be college ready. By understanding that students may disclose in different ways, student affairs educators are challenged to shape environments responsive to students' needs.

For example, consider how being aware of working-class students and students with disabilities might encourage educators to proactively examine the following questions: What are the costs associated with academic supplies (e.g., textbooks, software) and cocurricular involvement (e.g., dues, activities)? What types of assistance are available to eliminate, lower, or cover those costs? How accessible is the environment of a class, cocurricular activity, residence hall, or campus office? Are there different ways to access information, such as course content or student staff development activities? Are there multiple ways to demonstrate understanding, whether through multiple types of assignments or flexible design in interviews for student staff positions? Is there flexibility in absence or time-off policies to account for emergencies that might arise for students? Staff, faculty, and administrators can consider these questions the start of an equity audit, whether formal or informal, to examine the inclusivity and accessibility of their institutions. By learning to conduct these types of audits and work toward equity, educators develop proactive interventions that support students across marginalized identities.

Additionally, institutions often use formal measurements (e.g., registering with the office of disability services; using expected family contributions to calculate financial aid packages) to recognize which students may need resources. However, as students' identities are not stagnant, these strategies may not support students diagnosed with disabilities during college or whose class status changes during college. In other cases, students might see disability or working-class (alternatively, first-generation or low-income status) as institutionally defined and not representative of their personal experience (e.g., Bettencourt et al., 2020); there may be cases where need emerges past the typical orientation period, or an individual does not consider themselves eligible for resources. Thus, systems can create barriers that prevent students from getting access to or learning about resources.

While I frame many of these implications on lessening the need for disclosure, it is important to note that disclosure can be valuable. For example, many students from marginalized groups benefit from opportunities to be in community with others who share their identities (e.g., Bettencourt, 2020a; Patton, 2010). These resources should also be fostered with the recognition that staff should be trained comprehensively in resources and supports on campus. Do resources for first-generation students include information about registering with disability services? Vice versa? Moreover, the idea of interconnectivity shown through identity disclosure shows that affinity spaces might also be created around shared experiences. For example, a workshop titled "How to Communicate With Faculty" might support both students with disabilities and working-class students who may need to navigate different barriers in classes. The shared experience might also apply to other groups as well, such as international students who may be learning the norms of communication with faculty in the United States compared to their home countries.

Finally, students with disabilities and working-class students often feel pressure to downplay or erase identities to participate in higher education, to connect with peers, and avoid stigma (Abes & Wallace, 2018; Hurst, 2010; Stuber, 2011). However, disclosure can also be an act of empowerment. For example, writing activities where marginalized students share their experiences have been found to benefit a sense of belonging, the ability to see multiple perspectives, and individual learning (Chandler, 2002; Jehangir, 2010). Such acts can encourage meaning-making (Baxter Magolda, 2008) as students grapple with external messages about identity that may be deficit-based and instead develop internal frameworks. In a study on working-class students at public research universities (Bettencourt, 2020b), I found that participants with higher levels of meaning-making were more likely to describe strengths and assets associated with their social class backgrounds. Creating opportunities for students to share their identities in communities that can support and recognize their assets may be empowering opportunities for students with disabilities and working-class students.

CONCLUSION

Many students like Avery and Sam navigate through higher education each year in the United States. While ableism and classism uniquely frame the experiences of each student, the shared experience of disclosure creates valuable opportunities to build empathy and understanding. For student affairs, encouraging educators to compare and analyze these experiences can create deeper learning on several levels—understanding the concept of disclosure; generating strategies to support students with disabilities and working-class students individually; and developing a proactive approach to lessening barriers in higher education that can promote equity and social justice. The power of identity interconnections creates these opportunities to engage with the similarities and differences of shared experiences and to build coalitions through understanding.

REFERENCES

Abes, E. S., & Wallace, M. M. (2018). "People see me, but they don't see me:" An intersectional study of college students with physical disabilities. *Journal of College Student Development, 59*(5), 545–562. https://doi.org/10.1343/csd.2018.0052

Americans With Disabilities Act of 1990, 42 U.S.C. § 12101 *et seq.* (1990). https://www.ada.gov/pubs/adastatute08.htm

Ardoin, S., & martinez, b. (2019). *Straddling class in the academy: 26 stories of students, administrators, and faculty from poor and working-class backgrounds and their compelling lessons for higher education policy and practice.* Stylus.

Armstrong, E. A., & Hamilton, L. T. (2013). *Paying for the party: How college maintains inequality.* Harvard University Press.

Barratt, W. (2011). *Social class on campus: Theories and manifestations.* Stylus.

Baxter Magolda, M. B. (2008). Three elements of self-authorship. *Journal of College Student Development, 49*(4), 269–284. https://doi.org/10.1353/csd.0.0016

Bettencourt, G. M. (2020a). "You can't be a class ally if you're an upper-class person because you don't understand": Working-class students' definitions and perceptions of social class allyship. *Review of Higher Education, 44*(2), 265–291. https://doi.org/10.1353/rhe.2020.0041

Bettencourt, G. M. (2020b). "When I think about working-class, I think about people that work for what they have": How working-class students engage in meaning-making about their social class identity. *Journal of College Student Development, 61*(2), 22–38. https://doi.org/10.1353/csd.2020.0015

Bettencourt, G. M., Kimball, E., & Wells, R. S. (2018). Disability in postsecondary STEM learning environments: What faculty focus groups reveal about definitions and obstacles to effective support. *Journal of Postsecondary Education and Disability, 31*(4), 387–400. https://higherlogicdownload.s3.amazonaws.com/AHEAD/38b602f4-ec53-451c-9be0-5c0bf5d27c0a/UploadedImages/JPED/JPED_Volume_31/Issue_4/JPED_31_4__Final.pdf

Bettencourt, G. M., Mansour, K. E., Hedayet, M., Feraud-King, P. T., Stephens, K. J., Tejada, M. M., & Kimball, E. (2020, March 27). Is first-gen an identity? How first-generation college students make meaning of institutional and familial constructs of self. *Journal of College Student Retention: Research, Theory, & Practice.* https://doi.org/10.1177/1521025120913302

Carroll-Miranda, M. A. (2017). Access to higher education mediated by acts of self-disclosure: "It's a *hassle.*" In S. L. Kerschbaum, L. T. Eisenman, & J. M. Jones (Eds.), *Negotiating disability: Disclosure in higher education* (pp. 275–290). University of Michigan Press.

Castañeda, C., Hopkins, L. E., & Peters, M. L. (2010). Introduction. In M. A. Adams, W. J. Blumenfeld, C. Castañeda, H. W. Hackman, M. L. Peters, & X. Zúñiga (Eds), *Readings for diversity and social justice* (2nd ed., pp. 457–464). Routledge.

Chandler, G. E. (2002). An evaluation of college and low-income youth writing together: Self-discovery and cultural connection. *Issues in Comprehensive Pediatric Nursing, 25*(4), 255–269. https://doi.org/10.1080/01460860290042620

Chetty, R., Friedman, J. N., Saez, E., Turner, N., & Yagan, D. (2017). *Mobility report cards: The role of colleges in intergenerational mobility.* http://www.equality-of-opportunity.org/papers/coll_mrc_paper.pdf

Civil Rights Act of 1964, Pub. L. 88-352, 78 Stat. 241 (1964). https://www.govinfo.gov/content/pkg/STATUTE-78/pdf/STATUTE-78-Pg241.pdf

Dolmage, J. (2017). *Academic ableism: Disability and higher education.* University of Michigan Press.

Elkins, B., & Hanke, E. (2018). Code-switching to navigate social class in higher education. In G. L. Martin & B. Elkins (Eds.), *Social class identity in student affairs* (New Directions for Student Services, no. 162, pp. 35–47). Jossey-Bass. https://doi.org/10.1002/ss.20260

Fox, J. R., Park, B., & Lang, A. (2007). When available resources become negative resources: The effects of cognitive overload on memory sensitivity and criterion bias. *Communication Research, 34*(3), 277–296. https://doi.org/10.1177/0093650207300429

Freie, C. (2007). *Class construction: White working-class student identity in the new millennium.* Lexington Books.

Garrison, Y. L., & Liu, W. M. (2018). Using the social class worldview model in student affairs. In G. L. Martin & B. Elkins (Eds.), *Social class identity in student affairs* (New Directions for Student Services, no. 162, pp. 19–33). https://dx.doi.org/10.1002/ss.20259

Harper, S. R., Wardell, C. C., & McGuire, K. M. (2011). Man of multiple identities: Complex individuality and identity intersectionality among college men. In J. A. Laker & T. Davis (Eds.), *Masculinities in higher education: Theoretical and practical considerations* (pp. 81–96). Taylor & Francis. https://doi.org/10.4324/9780203833056

Hong, B. S. S. (2015). Qualitative analysis of the barriers college students with disabilities experience in higher education. *Journal of College Student Development, 56*(3), 209–226. https://doi.org/10.1353/csd.2015.0032

hooks, b. (2000). *Where we stand: Class matters.* Routledge.

Hurst, A. L. (2010). *The burden of academic success: Managing working-class identities in college.* Lexington Books.

Individuals With Disabilities Education Improvement Act of 2004, P.L. 108–446 (2004)

Jack, A. A. (2019). *The privileged poor: How elite colleges are failing disadvantaged students.* Harvard University Press.

Jehangir, R. (2010). Stories as knowledge: Bringing the lived experience of first-generation college students into the academy. *Urban Education, 45*(4), 533–553. https://doi.org/10.1177/0042085910372352

Karabel, J. (2006). *The chosen: The hidden history of admission and exclusion at Harvard, Yale, and Princeton.* Marliner Books.

Keating, A. (2013) *Transformation now! Towards a post-oppositional politics of change.* University of Illinois Press.

Kezar, A., Kitchen, J., Estes, H., Hallett, R., & Perez, R. (2020). Tailoring programs to best support low-income, first-generation, and racially minoritized college student success. *Journal of College Student Retention.* https://doi.org/https://doi.org/10.1177/1521025120971580

Kimball, E. W., Wells, R. S., Ostiguy, B. J., Manly, C. A., & Lauterbach, A. A. (2016). Students with disabilities in higher education: A review of the literature and an agenda for future research. In M. Paulsen (Ed.), *Higher education: Handbook of theory and research* (pp. 91–156). Springer. http://dx.doi.org/10.1007/978-3-319-26829-3_3

Leondar-Wright, B., & Yeskel, F. (2007). Classism curriculum design. In M. Adams, L. A. Bell, & P. Griffin (Eds.), *Teaching for diversity and social justice* (2nd ed., pp. 309–333). Routledge.

Lott, B. (2002). *American Psychologist, 57*(2), 100–110. https://doi.org/10.1037/0003-066X.57.2.100

Lott, B. (2012). The social psychology of class and classism. *American Psychologist, 67*(8), 650–658. https://doi.org/10.1037/a0029369

Mamisheishvili, K., & Koch, L. C. (2011). First-to-second-year persistence of students with disabilities in postsecondary institutions in the United States, *Rehabilitation Counseling Bulletin, 54*(2), 93–105. https://doi.org/10.1177/0034355210382580

Markoulakis, R., & Kirsh, B. (2013). Difficulties for university students with mental health problems: A critical interpretive synthesis. *The Review of Higher Education, 37*(1), 77–100. https://doi.org/10.1353/rhe.2013.0073

McNair, T. B., Albertine, S., Cooper, M. A., McDonald, N., & Major, T., Jr. (2016). *Becoming a student-ready college: A new culture of leadership for student success.* Jossey-Bass.

Miller, R. A., Wynn, R. D., & Webb, K. W. (2017). Complicating "coming out:" Disclosing disability, gender, and sexuality in higher education. In S. L. Kerschbaum, L. T. Eisenman, & J. M. Jones (Eds.), *Negotiating disability: Disclosure in higher education* (pp. 115–134). University of Michigan Press.

Miller, R. A., Wynn, R. D., & Webb, K. W. (2019). "This really interesting juggling act": How university students manage disability/queer identity disclosure and visibility. *Journal of Diversity in Higher Education, 12*(4), 307–318. http://dx.doi.org/10.1037/dhe0000083

Nguyen, T. H., & Nguyen, B. M. D. (2018). Is the "first-generation student" term useful for understanding inequality? The role of intersectionality in illuminating the implication of an accepted—yet unchallenged—term. *Review of Research in Education, 42,* 146–176. http://doi.org/10.3102/0091732X18759280

Patton, L. D. (Ed.). (2010). *Cultural centers in higher education: Perspectives on identity, theory, and practice.* Stylus.

Piketty, T. (2014). *Capital in the twenty-first century.* Harvard University Press.

Servicemen's Readjustment Act of 1944. Pub. L. 346. (1944)

Shakespeare, T. (2012). Still a health issue. *Disability and Health Journal, 5*(3), 129–131. https://doi.org/10.1016/j.dhjo.2012.04.002

Snyder, T. D., de Bray, C., & Dillow, S. A. (2019). *Digest of education statistics, 2017* (NCED 2018-070). https://nced.ed.gov/pubsearch/pubsinfo.asp?pubid= 2018070

Stich, A. E., & Freie, C. (2016). Introduction: The working-classes and higher education: An introduction to a complicated relationship. In A. E. Stich & C. Freie (Eds.), *The working-classes and education: Inequality of access, opportunity, and outcome* (pp. 1–10). Routledge.

Stuber, J. M. (2011). *Inside the college gates: How class and culture matter in higher education.* Lexington Books.

Thelin, J. R. (2019). *A history of American higher education* (3rd ed.). Johns Hopkins University Press.

Toutkoushian, R. K., Stollberg, R. A., & Slaton, K. A. (2018). Talking 'bout my generation: Defining "first-generation college students" in higher education research. *Teachers College Record, 120*(4), 1–38. https://www.tcrecord.org/Content .asp?ContentId=22042

7

Too Much and Not Enough

Exploring Identity Interconnections Between Biracial and Bisexual Students in Higher Education

Rebecca Cepeda and Kaity Prieto

Who, me confused? Ambivalent? Not so. Only your labels split me.

—Anzaldúa, 2015, p. 205

BISEXUAL AND BIRACIAL individuals may experience feelings of being "betwixt-and-between" because of the existing systems of power that assume singular conceptualizations of social identities (Ralston et al., 2017). The emphasis on the singularity of identity—and the monoracism and monosexism that results from this way of thinking—creates a false notion of what it means to be "enough." This chapter explores the utility of engaging identity interconnections between bisexual and biracial identity, both to promote allyship between biracial and bisexual people, as well as to foster identity exploration among individuals. We begin with the recognition that sexuality and racial identity are only two distinctive dimensions of identity. Students' socially constructed identities are multiple and intersecting, and these identities vary in salience across time and context (Abes et al., 2007; Jones & Abes, 2013). We use Keating's

99

(2013) notion of "shared commonality (not sameness)" to explore the way commonalities allow for the recognition of difference *and* points of connection (p. 11). In addition, we embrace Keating's (2013) rejection of binary thinking, which is appropriate for liminal identities (e.g., bisexuality, biracial identity) which defy binaries.

To engage in this discussion on biracial and bisexual identity interconnections, we delve into the relevant literature on bisexual, biracial, and bisexual/biracial students in higher education, with a focus on critical and poststructural approaches. We emphasize systems of power, privilege, and oppression and recognize the liminal, or in-between, nature of biracial and bisexual identity. Furthermore, we present our personal narratives as biracial and bisexual individuals as a starting point for community and empathy building and identify similarities across our identities while also noting the key differences—and the distinct social structures that give rise to those differences. It is critical that we not be reductive in our framing of commonality lest we erase the painful realities of racism and bi-negativity that uniquely shape our experiences. Conversely, we cannot ignore the privileges we hold, and we encourage those working with students to reflect on this as well. We conclude with implications for student affairs educators who wish to employ identity interconnections within their practices. Engaging with identity interconnections can facilitate student learning and development for biracial and bisexual students in higher education.

REVIEW OF THE LITERATURE

This section establishes a shared understanding of these student communities by first exploring the existing scholarship on bisexual and biracial students in higher education. Moreover, we acknowledge that individuals may be both bisexual and biracial; therefore, we also examine literature that encompasses these intersecting identities.

Bisexuality and Monosexism

Bisexuality is "an umbrella term for people who recognize and honor their potential for sexual and emotional attraction to more than one gender" (Bisexual Resource Center, 2019, para. 2). This definition of bisexuality overlaps considerably with terms like *pansexual*, which refers to the attraction to people regardless of their gender identity (Hayfield, 2020). Individuals who do not identify as monosexual may use the term *pansexual*, *bisexual*, both, or neither; other less common but equally valid labels include *omnisexual,* *plurisexual,* and *fluid,* among many others. Each term carries with it a distinct meaning, which may vary somewhat from person to person.

Bisexual individuals make up the largest portion of the LGBTQ+ community (Gates, 2011), with recent estimates indicating that 11.4% of college students identify as bisexual, with an additional 2.1% and 1.8% identifying as pansexual and queer, respectively (American College Health Association, 2020). Nevertheless, limited scholarship has explored bisexual student identity and experience (Monro et al., 2017). Despite a lack of higher education research centering bisexual students, the campus climate literature has suggested LGBTQ+ students continue to experience an unwelcoming campus environment (Blumenfeld et al., 2016; Tetreault et al., 2013), although conditions may be slowly improving (Beemyn & Rankin, 2011).

It is unsurprising that campus contexts may be hostile to bisexual students, given the various forms of oppression shaping bisexual student experiences. Bisexual and pansexual students experience heterosexism (Cramer, 2011), monosexism (Eisner, 2013), and bisexual erasure (Jones & Hillier, 2014; Yoshino, 2000). They may have their identities invalidated, or the existence of bisexuality questioned (Bradford, 2004). Bisexual students also struggle to identify role models on campus (Lowy, 2017) or access campus programming specific to their needs (Fine, 2012; Tavarez, 2020).

Monosexism on the college campus obscures the need for bi-inclusive resources and communicates to these students that their presence on campus is not valued (Lowy, 2017). Bisexual and pansexual students also experience exclusion from both gay and straight campus communities (Lowy, 2017; Prieto Godoy, 2020). They must situationally negotiate their bisexual or pansexual identity to find safety and belonging, at times downplaying their sexuality and at other times attempting to make it more visible (Prieto Godoy, 2020). It can be difficult for bi and pan individuals to make their identity visible given the liminal nature of these sexualities, in which "the margins of difference are blurred and manipulated in ways that scripted interactions are rendered seemingly unstable or inarticulate" (LeMaster, 2011, p. 107). To further consider the identity interconnections among bisexual and biracial students in higher education, next, we explore scholarship on biracial identity.

Biraciality and Monoracism

Biracial "refers to a person whose parents are of two different socially designated racial groups" while multiracial "refers to people who are of two or more racial heritages . . . [including] biracial people" (Root, 1996, p. xi). Biracial and multiracial may be used distinctly or interchangeably depending on individual preferences.

According to the U.S. Census, approximately 10 million individuals identify as multiracial, encompassing approximately 3% of the U.S. population (U.S. Census Bureau, 2017). By the year 2050, the multiracial population is projected to comprise 20% of the U.S. population (Lee & Bean, 2004). As the multiracial population continues to increase, it is assumed that the number of multiracial students in higher education will also increase.

Within the field of higher education, scholarship has highlighted how environments influence multiracial students and their racial identity. For example, Root (1996) suggested that multiracial individuals may have the opportunity to engage in border crossings where "one can bridge the border by having both feet in both groups . . . crossing between and among social contexts defined by race and ethnicity" (p. xxi). Similarly, Renn (2000) observed how higher education environments influence multiracial college students and their racial identity, including students consciously shifting their racial identity depending on various circumstances and environments. Furthermore, recent scholarship has demonstrated that biracial and multiracial students experience racial discrimination on college campuses (Harris, 2017; Kellogg & Liddell, 2012; Museus et al., 2016) and monoracism, a form of oppression on a systemic or interpersonal level based on not fitting into one racial category (Johnston-Guerrero & Nadal, 2010). For example, multiracial students often felt as if their race was questioned by monoracial students who either identified with a group within one of their racial identities or monoracial students who did not share a racial identity with them (Kellogg & Liddell, 2012). Harris (2017) revealed that multiracial students experienced a denial of their multiracial identity where "monoracial individuals were aware of multiracial women students' multiple racial identities but refused to acknowledge them" (p. 437).

Biracial and multiracial students are often assumed to experience privilege because of their ability to situationally racially identify (Campbell, 2009) or be disregarded in college campus programming that focuses on addressing racial issues through monoracial lenses (Literte, 2010). Biracial and multiracial students racially identify differently over time, moving and flowing through various racial identity patterns (Renn, 2004). Although we center this chapter on examining commonalities between bisexual and biracial students, we further acknowledge that individuals may be both bisexual and biracial. Therefore, we offer existing literature on this specific intersectional identity.

The Intersection of Identity

> Perhaps my identity oscillates at times, but in a world that attempts to force me to choose one side of a binary, I remain firmly in the middle. I cannot and will not choose just one thing. I won't erase any part of me. After years of struggling to answer the questions, "What are you?" I have finally realized that I have an answer. I am biracial. I am bisexual. I am complete. (Auljay, 2020, para. 17)

In keeping with the recognition that identities are multiple and intersecting (Abes et al., 2007; Jones & McEwen, 2000), a much smaller body of literature has emerged recognizing that people can be *both* bisexual and biracial. For instance, King (2011) found the women in her study detailed how they developed their multiracial/biracial and bisexual/pansexual identities both separately and simultaneously. Importantly, participants did not necessarily become comfortable with both of their identities, and no student discussed a space in which they could explore the intersections of their sexuality and race simultaneously. As another study of bisexual-biracial women suggested, this may be due to the homogeneity of single identity-based organizations and the hegemony of whiteness in queer spaces (Thompson, 2012).

Yet others have indicated that holding one bi identity might help to find comfort and meaning in the other. Israel (2004) described how her bisexual identity helped her reconcile her Chinese American and Jewish American identities, and Dworkin (2002) detailed how biracial and bicultural identities helped women accept their bisexuality. Further, people who identify as bisexual/plurisexual and biracial/multiracial may also identify positive aspects of their intersecting identities, namely their uniqueness, access to numerous experiences and communities, and their sense of pride (Galupo et al., 2019). Aside from King's (2011) work, scholars have not centered the bisexual and biracial college student experience. What is apparent, however, is the difficulty of finding a place to belong but also the importance of space—physical and psychological—for identity exploration (King, 2011; Renn, 2000, 2003). In relation to building empathy and bridging bisexual and biracial identities, we reflect on how we have built community with one another and share our narratives as bisexual and biracial individuals.

FINDING COMMUNITY AMONG THE IN BETWEEN

We cultivated a relationship with one another as we both worked within the same office for our graduate research assistantships and enrolled in the same higher education and students affairs doctoral program at The Ohio State University. Rebecca was a first-year PhD student and Kaity was a fourth-year PhD candidate. As we continued to learn more about one another, we shared our experiences with our biracial and bisexual identities, inspiring us to examine the similarities and differences between the two. We begin our exploration of the identity interconnections between bisexuality and biracial identity through our personal narratives, as it is our own identities and experiences that brought us to this work. In keeping with Keating's (2013) distinction between commonality and sameness, we emphasize that bisexuality and biraciality are not the same, *and* we can identify similarities and meaningful differences—both in the literature reviewed previously and in our dialogue.

Kaity's Narrative

Identities, although shaped by social institutions, are deeply personal. When I interview a research participant about their bisexual+ identity, I begin by asking what the term *bisexuality* means to them. It seems only fitting, then, that I begin my narrative the same way. For me, bisexuality is the attraction to people of any gender or of no gender, which is different from saying the gender of my partner does not matter. Gender matters to me—it shapes the way I experience the world, and it plays a role in my attraction to others.

There was never any doubt that in my mind that I am bisexual. While I may not have had a word to assign to my romantic and sexual desires, I have felt this way as long as I can remember. I never feared the crushes I had on women, but I had a general sense they would not be accepted. In middle and high school, my bisexuality was seen more as a curiosity, as though I was claiming this identity for attention, particularly from straight men. In college, it became an impediment to dating (some) queer women concerned that my interest in them was not genuine. There were moments where it was easier to selectively identify as gay or straight depending on context, despite being neither.

I deeply value my queer identity, and despite not feeling fully embraced by the queer community, I would never wish away my queerness. That said, there have been many moments where I hoped that I could simply be gay so that my queerness would not be questioned or invalidated. At the same time, I also recognize that being perceived as straight affords me a sense of safety. I appreciate that this is not the reality of many queer people, but I do not always experience passing as a privilege; it is painful to have an important part of my identity erased. This is a tension that I am still working to unpack.

Over the years, I have struggled with the validity of my sexuality because of these experiences. I experience frustration at not feeling straight enough for my heterosexual peers or queer enough for the LGBTQ+ community. I am constantly assumed to be an ally of LGBTQ+ people but never queer myself.

My understanding of my bisexual identity has changed because of my graduate school experiences. The scholarship I encountered during my master's program showed me that my experiences were not unusual. I learned that dedicated programming designed to support bisexual+ students is not common on college campuses, and I realized I owed it to myself to be open about who I am and advocate for students like me. I feel at home in my research, and my scholarship affords me a sense of visibility. Now, I feel joy in my sexuality. With my parents, my partner, my friends, and collaborators of all sexualities, I feel seen, and I feel affirmed. Most importantly, I feel loved—not for "both parts" of me but for all of me.

Rebecca's Narrative

I am a product of my Filipino mother and my Mexican father, both of whom immigrated to the United States because of the popularized ideas of living a life of freedom and opportunity in this country. My parents' differences in racial and ethnic identities have shaped how I navigate the world as a biracial individual. I have experienced both frustrations and joys with my biracial identity. I have experienced frustrations with not feeling "enough" within either of my racial communities in how I physically look and the fact that I am neither fluent in Spanish nor Tagalog. However, I have also experienced joys learning about my ancestors' histories and their active engagement in resistance within inequitable political climates. Moreover, I have felt pride in how my parents have experienced criticisms for their interracial relationship and have been determined to continue to love one another despite these judgments.

My understanding of my biracial identity has changed because of my experience in higher education. Being biracial on a college campus as an undergraduate student made me feel excluded in the recruitment of racial organizations because I questioned my racial authenticity and felt as if I was not Filipino or Mexican "enough" (Ashlee & Quaye, 2020). However, during my master's program, I was exposed to scholarship about multiracial students in a student development course. I felt seen. I felt heard. Without graduate school, I am unsure whether I would have discovered literature or would have the language to describe how my identity has changed over time. For example, I situationally identified with one race over the other depending on the context of my environment. I identified as Mexican American in spaces where I was surrounded by Latinx communities and Filipino American in spaces where I was surrounded by Asian communities. Doing so provided me the opportunity to attempt to prove my racial authenticity to my different monoracial communities. However, there were other environments in which I identified with both of my racial identities (Renn, 2004). I identified as both Mexican and Filipino when I encountered multiethnic or multiracial individuals because I felt a sense of acceptance for my multiracial identity. Later, I came across Guevarra's (2012) scholarship on Mexipino identity that validated my experiences as someone who is both Mexican and Filipino and empowered me to ultimately identify as Mexipina. Moreover, Root's (1996) Bill of Rights for Racially Mixed People has continued to remind me to embrace my biracial identity, stop trying to prove my racial authenticity to others, and remind myself that I am enough.

Reflecting on and Exploring Our Identity Interconnections

After reading one another's narratives through a lens of interconnectivity (Keating, 2013), we each crafted an individual response exploring the similarities and differences we observed between our personal experiences. We remained in conversation as we wrote, checking in with one another to deepen our understandings and celebrate one another's stories. Furthermore, we reflected on our experiences as we engaged in this dialogue.

Rebecca's Response
I observe similarities between my biracial narrative and your bisexual narrative and how we consider our identities as opposed to how others perceive us. For example, I noticed you expressed how there was never any doubt that you are bisexual. However, others perceived your bisexuality to be ingenuine or an attempt to seek attention. I resonate with the feeling of fully understanding and appreciating my biracial identity as a Mexipina yet being invalidated by others and questioned about being racially "enough." I recognize that we

have both questioned the validity of our identities because we do not fit into one assumed box or category related to sexuality or race.

I also noticed the role that graduate education played in our understandings of our identities. The scholarship we both encountered in our master's programs provided us both with validation and language to describe our unique experiences. Additionally, I feel that we both show deep appreciation for learning about biraciality and bisexuality in graduate school because it encouraged us to embrace "both" and all that encompasses our "bi" identities.

Although we share parallels within our narratives, there are distinct differences in our narratives. For example, I have never experienced my sexuality being questioned by others or have been accused of seeking attention due to my romantic relationships or sexual attractions.

Kaity's Response

I was also struck by the similarities between our narratives, particularly around feeling invalidated by those around us. I found it troubling that neither of us felt a sense of belonging relative to our biracial or bisexual identities during undergrad. It was not until we started engaging with the literature that we started to feel valid—I am sitting with what that means for people who do not have access to higher education and wonder what other spaces might exist for this type of belonging and self-reflection to occur.

Something else that struck me was your use of the term *Mexipina* along with *biracial*. I relate this to my use of the term *queer* to capture my ontological and political orientation toward my identity but also call myself bisexual to stress that my queerness is not monosexual. Our conversation around this highlighted the importance of finding a term you can feel at home in. What is also interesting is that we both appreciate the complexities of race, ethnicity, gender, and sexuality, and yet we also both use terms with the "bi" prefix—despite some criticism of these terms as reinforcing a binary (Gonel, 2013).

Of course, some differences between our experiences immediately jumped out to me as well. As a White, U.S.-born woman, I will never have to navigate the complexities of language or migration that you highlight in your narrative. I will never experience racism. My whiteness affords me access to many queer spaces that are not welcoming to People of Color. And although bisexual people must contend with the assumption that they are promiscuous, I recognize that my whiteness insulates me from this as well; as the discourse surrounding promiscuity has particular relevance for those who have been minoritized on the basis of race, ethnicity, and class (Cohen, 1996; Klesse, 2005).

Exploring Commonalities and Celebrating Differences

Engaging in dialogue and exploring commonalities and differences among our narratives has validated our experiences and feelings of being in-between. Moreover, it reminded us of Moraga's (2015) scholarship on racial identity and how building connections among one another is critical for the revolution against dominant and oppressive powers. Moraga (2015) wrote, "but one voice is not enough, nor two, although this is where dialogue begins. . . . Because my/your solitary, self-asserting 'go-for the throat-of-fear' power is not enough. The real power, as you and I well know, is collective" (p. 29). We each have experienced marginalization. Exploring our differences has highlighted the privileges we have and how we can be allies to one another. Specifically centering and relating our narratives is a form of collectivity and resistance against the oppressive forces we face as biracial and bisexual individuals.

Complex Interconnections

As our dialogue suggests, the identity interconnections between bisexuality and biracial identity are rich in both "points of *complex* connections" as well as important distinctions (Keating, 2013, p. 4). Our personal experiences served as a starting point in our theorizing how bisexual and biracial students might experience the world and how they might benefit from recognizing the interconnectivity of their distinct identities. In this section, we expand upon both and explore how identity interconnections between biracial and bisexual students may create opportunities for identity development, empathy building, and connectivity.

Meaningful Distinctions

Differences in how students experience their identities arise because the underlying systems of power shaping those experiences are distinct (i.e., monosexism and heteronormativity for White bisexual students versus the racism, monoracism, nativism, and xenophobia facing heterosexual, biracial students). Further, students' multiple dimensions of identity differentially shape their individual experiences and the meaning they make of those experiences (Abes et al., 2007). For instance, a Black pansexual woman may find connection with a queer woman who identifies as Black and Asian differently than she would with a heterosexual man who identifies as White and Latino. In this example, the two women might bond over their experiences with anti-Blackness and transgressing heteronormativity, whereas all three might have a shared experience with feeling "betwixt-and-between" multiple monosexual and/or monoracial groups (Ralston et al., 2017, p. 20). And our experiences as young women with "betwixt-and-between" racial and sexual identities have allowed us to bond over navigating gendered oppression in academia and the ways that oppression is complicated by race and sexuality. However, it is also critical to consider compassionate forms of caution when drawing a connection between shared experiences; similarities across groups should not be used to reinforce hierarchies of oppression or lead to competition among marginalized groups, as can occur when identity interconnections are not carefully facilitated (Tran & Johnston-Guerrero, 2016; we elaborate on this ethical consideration in the next section on implications for student affairs practice).

Additionally, some identities are invisible, while others are hyper-visible. For example, the often-invisible nature of sexuality permits bisexual students the opportunity to navigate heteronormative campus spaces by selectively disclosing their sexual identity only when they feel safe in doing so (Prieto Godoy, 2020). Whereas biracial students, particularly those who identify with two or more minoritized racial or ethnic identities, may feel marked as "other" by the color of their skin. Bisexual Students of Color may feel highly visible in their racial identities, particularly on a predominantly White campus, and prefer not to invite more unwanted attention by also being visibly queer (Prieto Godoy, 2020).

Points of Connection

And yet, this (in)visibility manifests as a point of connection as well. Carrillo Rowe (2008) refers to people "whose hues are read in ways we cannot predict, cannot control—by White people as the color of 'one of us,' by people of color as the color of dominance" (p. xix). Her words speak to the ways biracial people cannot control the assumptions made about them. She goes on—"How will we, the ones you can't tell about, make ourselves known?" (Carrillo Rowe, 2008, p. xix). These comments echo the voices of bisexual students who struggle to make themselves visible within the bounds of het-eronormative, monosexist culture (Prieto Godoy, 2020). Both biracial and bisexual students may be accused of or perceived to be passing, which refers to the enactment of identity in such a way that provides access to otherwise unobtainable benefits (Verni, 2009). Passing can serve as an intentional strat-egy to find safety and belonging, but it can also manifest as an undesired consequence of bisexual erasure and monoracism.

Points of connection also include feeling "betwixt-and-between" (Ralston et al., 2017, p. 20), or what Carrillo Rowe (2008) called being "split by cat-egories, by worlds and words" (p. xix). Biracial and bisexual people report not fitting in, feeling too much of one thing or not enough of another, and expe-riencing guilt associated with "choosing a side" (Bradford, 2004; Brittian et al., 2013; Prieto Godoy, 2020). For biracial and bisexual people, often women and queer people, being targets of sexual fetishization is another point of connection (Li et al., 2013; Renn, 2011).

Many of these common experiences of disconnection and erasure are rooted in "an overemphasis on narrow definitions of difference and iden-tity, defined in exclusionary, either/or terms" (Keating, 2013, p. 4). Keating's (2013) notion of "radical interconnectedness" may help mitigate these feel-ings of exclusion by moving beyond a separatist identity politics and embrac-ing interconnectedness (p. 30). In the remainder of this chapter, we explore opportunities for alliance-making, and empathy building between biracial and bisexual individuals, inspired by Women of Color feminisms, and point to ways student affairs educators can facilitate those connections (Anzaldúa, 2015; Carrillo Rowe, 2008; Keating, 2013).

Opportunities for Identity Exploration, Empathy, and Community Building

We encourage exploring similarities and differences because creating space for dialogue and identity exploration fosters identity development (see King, 2011; Renn, 2000, 2004). For instance, King (2011) acknowledged that campus experiences and interactions, including those between students with similar identities, offered students greater awareness of multiracial and bisexual identity. Spaces in which students could interact with "like-minded and sometimes like-appearing or like-experienced others" allowed students to make meaning of their race and sexuality (King, 2011, p. 450). Students benefit from spaces in which they find their identities affirmed and legiti-mized, yet formal spaces dedicated to biracial or bisexual students may be limited (Lowy, 2017; Renn, 2000). Further, there will always be some degree of difference in any affinity space given students' multiple identities. Yet as Renn (2000) found, even when multiracial students did not share the same ethnic or cultural backgrounds, a shared experience of navigating monoracial campuses as multiracial students nevertheless contributed to their sense of belonging. By bringing together biracial and bisexual students and emphasizing commonalities, student affairs educators can open up another space for identity exploration.

These spaces also allow for empathy, solidarity, and community building. Biracial and bisexual students both exist in liminal (i.e., transitory or in-between) spaces that defy binary thinking and leave open the possibility for transformation. Following Anzaldúa (2015), we suggest that biracial and bisexual students might lean into their need for connection and kinship. Carrillo Rowe's (2008) work on bridge methodology is instructive here. This approach facilitates alliance building by acknowledging difference, both between and within communities, and seeking commonality. Such an approach might require students to move beyond the assumptions underlying traditional identity labels (Keating, 2013). For example, a student may be surprised to learn that their bisexual peer is not only attracted to cisgender men and cisgender women, or that classmate who refers to themself as Black may also identify as biracial. As evidenced by our dialogue, this work entails asking questions and listening within an open heart. In the sections that follow we discuss how student affairs educators can intentionally create space for these conversations to take place.

IMPLICATIONS FOR STUDENT AFFAIRS PRACTICE

Identity interconnections can inform future student affairs research and practice through facilitating identity exploration, fostering solidarity across diverse groups, and advancing social justice. Recognizing commonalities and differences across social identities can cultivate a sense of connectedness and shared understanding when examining systems of power, privilege, and oppression. By encouraging the exploration of identity interconnections, higher education institutions can invite students to form allyships and build community across identities, which is significant for a student's sense of belonging and success on campus. Therefore, higher education institutions, faculty, and staff have an obligation to develop physical and virtual spaces for students to explore identity interconnections and build relationships across diverse groups of students. They must also ensure there are opportunities during classroom and cocurricular conversation for discussions of identity to occur.

To begin, we recommend institutional agents offer programming to build a bridge toward identity interconnections between biracial and bisexual students. For example, student affairs educators may encourage multiracial and bisexual students' organizations to host joint programming or organize book clubs by biracial and bisexual authors or with biracial and bisexual protagonists. Additionally, faculty members and student affairs educators might also consider bringing speakers to campus for a panel discussion centering biracial and bisexual experiences. By offering students opportunities to further explore their identities through interpersonal programming, students can construct connections with one another while understanding the differences between race and sexuality—and between racism, homophobia, and biphobia.

Furthermore, we recommend institutional agents facilitate intergroup dialogues between biracial and bisexual students in order to foster learning across social identities. According to Zúñiga (2003), "Intergroup dialogue is a face-to-face conversation between members of two or more social identity groups that strives to create new levels of understanding, relating, and action" (p. 9). A core element to intergroup dialogue is the exploration of social identities related to systemic inequalities (Maxwell et al., 2011). Furthermore, intergroup dialogue encompasses "active, experiential, and dialogic learning methods for students to engage in shared activities, stimulate conversation, foster critical thinking, and deepen dialogues" (Zúñiga et al., 2007, p. 91). Consequently, intergroup dialogues between biracial and bisexual students can offer a space for individuals to explore their own biracial or bisexual identities. Further, intergroup dialogues can cultivate levels of understanding that can potentially serve as a way for individuals to build allyship across identities by examining and bridging systemic inequities, such as monosexism and monoracism. Students may feel less alone in their experiences as they begin to recognize the tendency for U.S. society to view race, sexuality, and many other identities in binary terms. They may also feel empowered to speak up in the face of oppression, advocating not only for their own community but for their peers as well.

Ethical Considerations

We approach this topic with the assumption that student affairs educators seeking to engage this identity interconnection will do so with the intention of fostering social justice. Yet even the best intentions can lead to harm if conversations and programming are not approached with compassionate caution. In this section, we address the ethical considerations that apply to both the way we understand identity interconnections between biracial and bisexual students and our suggestions for practice.

As detailed throughout this chapter, we are proponents of leveraging identity interconnections to build community across difference and foster identity exploration. We offer a note of caution, however. Student affairs educators must take care not to essentialize a singular bisexual or biracial student experience. They must recognize that not everyone experiences their identities in the same way, acknowledging the distinctions of the histories between the identities and communities being explored (Tran & Johnston-Guerrero, 2016). Further, educators should make space for students who hold both biracial and bisexual identities. For instance, although a useful means of fostering solidarity across diverse groups, intergroup dialogues could inadvertently pressure a biracial, bisexual student to prioritize one dimension of their identity over another or to feel as though the intersection of their identities is being erased. Although this dialogue centers on two of their identities, a biracial, bisexual student may be unsure how to enter that space or conclude that they are, in fact, unwelcome. Conversely, they may feel obligated to serve as a bridge between these two communities. It is imperative that practitioners not frame the identity interconnection between bisexual and biracial identity in such a way that renders biracial, bisexual students invisible.

Although we believe in the need for open and thoughtful discussion of identity, we also caution against forcing students to engage in conversations that may feel unsafe. Not all students with minoritized identities—particularly invisible ones—will want to share. Historically, models of sexual identity development, for example, have culminated in identity disclosure and political activism (e.g., D'Augelli, 1994; Troiden, 1988). Critical and poststructural approaches to identity, however, emphasize the risks inherent in outness (Brockenbrough, 2015). For bisexual students with marginalized racial identities, de-emphasizing sexual identity is one way to navigate a racist campus environment (Prieto Godoy, 2020). Practitioners must appreciate that this is an important form of agency, and not pressure students to reveal more of themselves than they are comfortable.

Lastly, as we have argued throughout this chapter, it is critical that practitioners and students view identity interconnections as a heuristic device rather than an assertion that White bisexual students understand the racism and monoracism experienced by their biracial peers or that heterosexual biracial students now appreciate binegativity and monosexism. Further, students should be provided with opportunities to reflect on how they may participate in and perpetuate these respective and reinforcing forms of oppression. Moreover, student affairs educators must take care not to assume students who may experience their identities in analogous ways require the same resources or supports (Tran & Johnston-Guerrero, 2016).

CONCLUSION

As today's college students increasingly identify under the umbrella of bisexuality, biraciality, or as a combination of both, student affairs educators will need to intentionally design programming welcoming of these identities and experiences. One way they might do this is through embracing the interconnectedness of these liminal identities and fostering dialogue between and among biracial, bisexual, and biracial bisexual students in the interest of community building, alliance making, and identity exploration. Doing so requires intentional reflection and attention to ethical implications, but we argue this is a worthwhile pursuit.

REFERENCES

Abes, E. S., Jones, S. R., & McEwen, M. K. (2007). Reconceptualizing the model of multiple dimensions of identity: The role of meaning-making capacity in the construction of multiple identities. *Journal of College Student Development, 48*(1), 1–22. https://doi.org/ 10.1353/csd.2007.0000

American College Health Association. (2020). *American College Health Association-National College Health Assessment III: Undergraduate reference group executive summary spring 2020.* https://www.acha.org/documents/ncha/NCHA-III_Spring_2020_Undergraduate_Reference_Group_Executive_Summary.pdf

Anzaldúa, G. (2015). La P. In C. Moraga & G. Anzaldúa (Eds.), *This bridge called my back: Writings by radical women of color* (4th ed., pp. 198–209). State University of New York Press.

Ashlee, A. A., & Quaye, S. J. (2020). On being racially enough: A duoethnography across minoritized racial identities. *International Journal of Qualitative Studies in Education, 34*(3), 243–261. https://doi.org/10.1080/09518398.2020.1753256

Auljay, K. (2020, February 13). Always in the middle: On being biracial & bisexual. *Autostraddle.* https://www.autostraddle.com/always-in-the-middle-on-being-biracial-bisexual/

Beemyn, G., & Rankin, S. (2011). Introduction to the special issue on "LGBTQ campus experiences." *Journal of Homosexuality, 58*(9), 1159–1164. https://doi .org/10.1080/00918369.2011.605728

Bisexual Resource Center. (2019). *Welcome home.* https://biresource.org/

Blumenfeld, W. J., Weber, G. N., & Rankin, S. (2016). In our own voice: Campus climate as a mediating factor in the persistence of LGBT people in higher education. In E. A. Mikulec & P. C. Miller (Eds.), *Queering classrooms: Personal narratives and educational practices to support LGBTQ youth in schools* (pp. 187–212). Information Age.

Bradford, M. (2004). The bisexual experience: Living in a dichotomous culture. *Journal of Bisexuality, 4*(1–2), 7–23. https://doi.org/10.1300/J159v04n01_02

Brittian, A. S., Umaña-Taylor, A. J., & Derlan, C. L. (2013). An examination of biracial college youths' family ethnic socialization, ethnic identity, and adjustment: Do self-identification labels and university context matter? *Cultural Diversity and Ethnic Minority Psychology, 19*(2), 177–189. https://doi.org/10.1037/a0029438

Brockenbrough, E. (2015). Queer of color agency in educational contexts: Analytic frameworks from a queer of color critique. *Educational Studies, 51*(1), 28–44. https://doi.org/10.1080/00131946.2014.979929

Campbell, M. E. (2009). Multiracial groups and educational inequality: A rainbow or a divide? *Social Problems, 56*(3), 425–446. https://doi.org/10.1525/sp.2009.56.3.425

Carrillo Rowe, A. (2008). *Power lines: On the subject of feminist alliances.* Duke University Press.

Cohen, C. J. (1996). Contested membership: Black gay identities and the politics of AIDS. In S. Seidman (Ed.), *Queer theory/sociology* (pp. 362–395). Blackwell.

Cramer, E. P. (Ed.). (2011). *Addressing homophobia and heterosexism on college campuses.* Routledge.

D'Augelli, A. R. (1994). Identity development and sexual orientation: Toward a model of lesbian, gay, and bisexual development. In E. J. Trickett, R. J. Watts, & D. Birman (Eds.), *Human diversity: Perspectives on people in context* (pp. 312–333). Jossey-Bass.

Dworkin, S. H. (2002). Biracial, bicultural, bisexual: Bisexuality and multiple identities. *Journal of Bisexuality, 2*(4), 93–107. https://doi.org/10.1300/J159v02n04_06

Eisner, S. (2013). *Bi: Notes for a bisexual revolution.* Seal Press.

Fine, L. E. (2012). The context of creating space: Assessing the likelihood of college LGBT center presence. *Journal of College Student Development, 53*(2), 285–299. https://doi.org/10.1353/csd.2012.0017

Galupo, M. P., Taylor, S. M., & Cole, D., Jr. (2019). "I am double the bi": Positive aspects of being both bisexual and biracial. *Journal of Bisexuality, 19*(2), 152–168. https://doi.org/10.1080/15299716.2019.1619066

Gates, G. J. (2011). How many people are lesbian, gay, bisexual and transgender? *UCLA: The Williams Institute.* http://williamsinstitute.law.ucla.edu/wp-content/uploads/Gates-How-Many-People-LGBT-Apr-2011.pdf

Gonel, A. H. (2013). Pansexual identification in online communities: Employing a collaborative queer method to study pansexuality. *Graduate Journal of Social Science, 10*(1), 36–59. http://gjss.org/sites/default/files/issues/chapters/papers/Journal-10-01--02-HaleGonel.pdf

Guevara, R. P., Jr. (2012). *Becoming Mexipino: Multiethnic identities and communities in San Diego.* Rutgers University Press.

Harris, J. C. (2017). Multiracial college students' experiences with multiracial microaggressions. *Race Ethnicity and Education, 20*(4), 429–445. https://doi.org/10.1080/13613324.2016.1248836

Hayfield, N. (2020). *Bisexual and pansexual identities.* Routledge.

Israel, T. (2004). Conversations, not categories: The intersection of biracial and bisexual identities. *Women & Therapy, 27*(1–2), 173–184. https://doi.org/10.1300/J015v27n01_12

Johnston-Guerrero, M. P., & Nadal, K. L. (2010). Multiracial microaggressions: Exposing monoracism in everyday life and clinical practice. In D. W. Sue (Ed.), *Microaggressions and marginality: Manifestation, dynamics, and impact* (pp. 123–144). Wiley.

Jones, S. R., & Abes, E. S. (2013). *Identity development of college students: Advancing frameworks for multiple dimensions of identity.* Jossey-Bass.

Jones, S. R., & McEwen, M. K. (2000). A conceptual model of multiple dimensions of identity. *Journal of College Student Development, 41*(4), 405–416. https://www.researchgate.net/publication/292759031_A_conceptual_model_of_multiple_dimensions_of_identity

Jones, T., & Hillier, L. (2014). The erasure of bisexual students in Australian education policy and practice. *Journal of Bisexuality, 14*(1), 53–74. https://doi.org/10.1080/15299716.2014.872465

Keating, A. (2013). *Transformation now! Toward a post-oppositional politics of change.* University of Illinois Press.

Kellogg, A. H., & Liddell, D. L. (2012). "Not half but double": Exploring critical incidents in the racial identity of multiracial college students. *Journal of College Student Development, 53*(4), 524–541. https://doi.org/10.1353/csd.2012.0054

King, A. R. (2011). Environmental influences on the development of female college students who identify as multiracial/biracial-bisexual/pansexual. *Journal of College Student Development, 52*(4), 440–455. https://doi.org/10.1353/csd.2011.0050

Klesse, C. (2005). Bisexual women, non-monogamy and differentialist anti-promiscuity discourses. *Sexualities, 8*(4), 445–464. https://doi.org/10.1177/1363460705056620

Lee, J., & Bean, F. D. (2004). America's changing color lines: Immigration, race/ethnicity, and multiracial identification. *Annual Review of Sociology, 30,* 221–242. https://doi.org/10.1146/annurev.soc.30.012703.110519

LeMaster, B. (2011). Queer imag(in)ing: Liminality as resistance in Lindqvist's Let the Right One In. *Communication and Critical/Cultural Studies, 8*(2), 103–123. https://doi.org/10.1080/14791420.2011.566277

Li, T., Dobinson, C., Scheim, A. I., & Ross, L. E. (2013). Unique issues bisexual people face in intimate relationships: A descriptive exploration of lived experience. *Journal of Gay & Lesbian Mental Health, 17*(1), 21–39. https://doi.org/10.1080/19359705.2012.723607

Literte, P. E. (2010). Revising race: How biracial students are changing and challenging student services. *Journal of College Student Development, 51*(2), 115–134. https://doi:10.1353/csd.0.0122

Lowy, J. S. (2017). *Exploring bisexual women's experiences on college campuses* [Unpublished doctoral dissertation]. University of Georgia.

Maxwell, K. E., Chesler, M., & Nagda, B. A. (2011). Identity matters: Facilitators' struggles and empowered use of social identities in intergroup dialogue. In K. E. Maxwell, B. A. Nagda, & M. C. Thompson (Eds.), *Facilitating intergroup dialogues: Building differences, catalyzing change* (pp. 163–178). Stylus.

Monro, S., Hines, S., & Osborne, A. (2017). Is bisexuality invisible? A review of sexualities scholarship 1970–2015. *The Sociological Review, 65*(4), 663–681. https://doi.org/10.1177/0038026117695488

Moraga, C. (2015). La Güera. In C. Moraga & G. Anzaldúa (Eds.), *This bridge called my back: Writings by radical women of color* (4th ed.; pp. 22–29). State University of New York Press.

Museus, S. D., Lambe Sariñana, S. A., Yee, A. L., & Robinson, T. E. (2016). A qualitative analysis of multiracial students' experiences with prejudice and discrimination in college. *Journal of College Student Development, 57*(6), 680–697. https://doi.org/10.1353/csd.2016.0068

Prieto Godoy, K. A. (2020). *Bisexual college student's identity negotiation narratives* [Unpublished doctoral dissertation]. The Ohio State University.

Ralston, N. C., Nicolazzo, Z., & Harris, J. C. (2017). Betwixt–and–between: Counter-stories from the borderlands of higher education. *About Campus, 22*(4), 20–27. https://doi.org/10.1002/abc.21299

Renn, K. A. (2000). Patterns of situational identity among biracial and multiracial college students. *Review of Higher Education, 23*(4), 399–420. https://doi.org/10.1353/rhe.2000.0019

Renn, K. A. (2003). Understanding the identities of mixed race college students through a developmental ecology lens. *Journal of College Student Development, 44*(3), 383–403. https://doi.org/10.1353/csd.2003.0032

Renn, K. A. (2004). *Mixed race students in college: The ecology of race, identity, and community on campus.* State University of New York Press.

Renn, K. A. (2011). Biracial and multiracial college students. In M. J. Cuyjet, M. F. Howard-Hamilton, & D. L. Cooper (Eds.), *Multiculturalism on campus: Theories, models, and practices for understanding diversity and creating inclusion.* (pp. 191–212). Stylus.

Root, M. P. P. (1996). *The multiracial experience: Racial borders as the new frontier.* SAGE.

Tavarez, J. (2020). "I can't quite be myself": Bisexual-specific minority stress within LGBTQ campus spaces. *Journal of Diversity in Higher Education.* Advance online publication. https://doi.org/10.1037/dhe0000280

Tetreault, P. A., Fette, R., Meidlinger, P. C., & Hope, D. (2013). Perceptions of campus climate by sexual minorities. *Journal of Homosexuality, 60*(7), 947–964. https://doi.org/10.1080/00918369.2013.774874

Thompson, B. Y. (2012). The price of "community" from bisexual/biracial women's perspectives. *Journal of Bisexuality, 12*(3), 417–428. https://doi.org/10.1080/15299716.2012.702623

Tran, V. T., & Johnston-Guerrero, M. P. (2016). Is transracial the same as transgender? The utility and limitations of identity analogies in multicultural education. *Multicultural Perspectives, 18*(3), 134–139. https://doi.org/10.1080/15210960.2016.1186548

Troiden, R. R. (1988). *Gay and lesbian identity: A sociological analysis.* General Hall.

U.S. Census Bureau. (2017). *Selected race characteristics, 2013–2017 American Community Survey 5-year estimates.* https://factfinder.census.gov/faces/tableservices/jsf/pages/productview.xhtml?pid=ACS_17_5YR_B02001&prodType=table

Verni, R. (2009). Queering passing: An exploration of passing among GLBQ individuals. *Intersections: Women's and Gender Studies in Review Across Disciplines, 7*, 67–81. https://repositories.lib.utexas.edu/bitstream/handle/2152/11204/Intersections_issue_7.pdf#page=67

Yoshino, K. (2000). The epistemic contract of bisexual erasure. *Stanford Law Review*, *52*(2), 353–461. https://doi.org/10.2307/1229482

Zúñiga, X. (2003). Bridging differences through dialogue. *About Campus*, *7*(6), 8–16. https://doi.org/10.1177/108648220300700603

Zúñiga, X., Nagda, B. A., Chesler, M., & Cytron-Walker, A. (2007). Appendix: Educational resources. *ASHE Higher Education Report Series*, *32*(4), 91–118. Jossey-Bass. https://doi.org/10.1002/aehe.3204

8

Identity Interconnections Between Masculinity and Whiteness

A Tool for Developing Critical Consciousness and Inspiring Social Justice Action

Kyle C. Ashlee and Brandon Cash

NEARLY 30 YEARS AGO, feminist scholar and educator Peggy McIntosh (1988) published a working paper titled "White Privilege and Male Privilege: A Personal Account of Coming to See Correspondences Through Work in Women's Studies." In a way that had never been done before, this paper notably outlined dozens of specific examples of White privilege, or unearned advantages, that benefit White people and oppress People of Color. Since then, *The Privilege Knapsack* (McIntosh, 2008) has been named one of the most authoritative texts on the concept of White privilege and is cited as one of the catalysts for a mainstream conversation about White privilege around the world (Koch, 2012). In the field of higher education, McIntosh's work has become one of the most utilized teaching resources in helping individuals understand the idea of White privilege (Lensmire, 2013).

Although many student affairs educators are now familiar with McIntosh's seminal work on White privilege, few discuss the feminist origins of *The Privilege Knapsack*. The paper begins with McIntosh's testimony about the resistance she and other feminist educators experienced when attempting to educate men about their unexamined male privilege. She notes,

"Thinking through unacknowledged male privileges as a phenomenon, I realized that, since hierarchies in our society are interlocking, there was most likely a phenomenon of [W]hite privilege that was similarly denied and protected" (McIntosh, 1988, p. 1). In this quote, McIntosh describes how she came to realize her own White privilege through an already established understanding of male privilege. McIntosh drew from her understanding of power and privilege as a woman living within a patriarchal society to understand how White supremacy operates to benefit her as a White person. In other words, one of the most influential tools about White privilege ever created was developed through an *identity interconnection*.

The purpose of this chapter is to further explore identity interconnections between masculinity and whiteness, ultimately providing student affairs educators with a practical tool they can use to develop critical consciousness and inspire social justice action among individuals who hold dominant social identities. We frame this exploration through a lens of interconnectivity theory (Keating, 2013). By exploring Michael Kimmel's (2008) *Three Cultures of Guyland* and Ruth Frankenberg's (1993) *Three-Part Definition of Whiteness*, we establish an understanding of masculinity and whiteness, and offer differences and commonalities between these two dominant identities. Next, we examine our lived experiences as White men and describe how understanding identity interconnections between masculinity and whiteness helped us develop critical consciousness. Finally, we share practical possibilities related to identity interconnections between masculinity and whiteness to inform educators as they attempt to facilitate critical consciousness and inspire social justice action among individuals with dominant identities.

INTERCONNECTIVITY AS A THEORETICAL FRAMEWORK TO EXAMINE MASCULINITY AND WHITENESS

Keating (2013) describes interconnectivity as relational, meaning that this theoretical framework operates from the premise that all people, and the systems they live within, are interdependent and interconnected. In other words, interconnectivity provides a theoretical framework for understanding the interrelatedness of social identities and the interlocking nature of systems, like patriarchy and White supremacy, that privilege some while oppressing others. Rather than minimizing differences between identity experiences, interconnectivity positions differences across identity as sites for genuine connection to be built. It is only by practicing an ethic of interrelatedness, connecting through a process of exploring differences, and listening with raw openness that individuals with different identities can begin to forge authentic coalitions to advance social justice at the systemic level.

Given that interconnectivity theory was created out of Women of Color feminisms (Moraga & Anzaldúa, 2015), it is worth noting that the theory was not specifically intended to describe dominant experiences related to masculinity and whiteness. That said, we believe that interconnectivity provides a unique lens for examining the identity interconnection between masculinity and whiteness because it evaluates connections across inherited systems of power. While there are clear differences between masculinity and whiteness, the two identity experiences share striking commonalities related to power and privilege at the systemic level. Interconnectivity provides a useful framework for exploring these commonalities and differences because this framework is expansive, finding commonalities between seemingly contradictory identities, experiences, and systems (Keating, 2013). Throughout the rest of this chapter, we will use interconnectivity as a theoretical framework to examine identity interconnections between masculinity and whiteness. Interconnectivity will then frame the practical possibilities of using identity interconnections between masculinity and whiteness as a tool to develop critical consciousness and inspire social justice action among individuals who hold dominant identities.

Exploring the Differences and Commonalities Between Masculinity and Whiteness

To establish a foundation for exploring identity interconnections between masculinity and whiteness, we have identified two relevant and influential scholarly perspectives related to masculinity and whiteness. Michael Kimmel's (2008) *Three Cultures of Guyland* is a sociological analysis of masculinity that describes how patriarchy dictates men's behavior in college through a culture of entitlement, silence, and protection. Ruth Frankenberg's (1993) *Three-Part Definition of Whiteness* is a sociological model that characterizes how White supremacy manifests at the systemic, interpersonal, and individual levels. An analysis of these perspectives reveals that although there are notable differences between masculinity and whiteness, the two systems of power that undergird these identities—patriarchy and White supremacy—operate in strikingly similar ways, providing power and privilege to those with dominant identities while oppressing those who are marginalized. Conscious of our positionality as White men, our intention is not to exaggerate the differences between identities. Neither is their goal to assert that masculinity and whiteness are the same. Rather, exploring the differences and commonalities between masculinity and whiteness serves to highlight the underlying presence of power and privilege shared among these dominant identities and compels us to take action for social justice across all inherited systems of power.

Kimmel's Three Cultures of Guyland

Kimmel (2008) highlights three distinct yet interwoven cultural dynamics that comprise patriarchal masculinity in the United States, including a culture of entitlement, a culture of silence, and a culture of protection. Operating as a reward system for men, the culture of entitlement speaks to the inflated sense of assumed ownership associated with masculinity at the individual level. This culture emphasizes the notion that if a man follows the rules and works hard, he is entitled to the privileges of patriarchy, including power, influence, and control. Through a culture of silence, masculinity sustains the system of patriarchy at the interpersonal or group levels. Despite the ever-present fear fueled by patriarchy, men adhere to the culture of silence because it maintains the status quo in an environment that harshly punishes those who transgress traditional expressions of masculinity. The culture of protection expands beyond the individual and group dynamics to examine how patriarchal masculinity is reinforced at the systemic level. With the culture of entitlement fueling men's problematic behavior and the culture of silence providing complicit compliance, the culture of protection establishes a systemic shield of armor in which the destructive implications of masculinity are normalized and encouraged by men and others in society.

Frankenberg's Three-Part Definition of Whiteness

Frankenberg interviewed White women to ask them about their experiences with race, specifically from their childhoods, and discovered that the landscapes of these women's lives were largely structured by racism and privilege. Frankenberg (1993) defines whiteness as "a position of structural advantage," a "place from which to look at oneself, others and society," and "a set of cultural practices" for White people that is often unnamed, unacknowledged, and unexamined (p. 54). The first part of Frankenberg's definition outlines the systemic nature of whiteness as a structural advantage that applies to all White people at all times. The second part of the definition clarifies how whiteness operates as a social construct at the interpersonal level, allowing White people to feel as though they are individuals separate from institutions, objectively observing themselves and others, despite the ever-present quality of White supremacy. Finally, the last part of the definition describes the individual level by highlighting the cultural practices that individual White people enact, thus upholding and reinforcing White supremacy.

Differences Between Masculinity and Whiteness

Before exploring the commonalities between masculinity and whiteness, it is important to first acknowledge the very real differences between these two identity experiences. Given that interconnectivity insists on holding differences and commonalities across identity experiences, noting the differences between masculinity and whiteness is crucial. Doing so encourages readers, and us, to affirm the specific and unique characteristics of oppression experienced by those who are marginalized by patriarchy and White supremacy, respectively. Although there are many historical and cultural differences between how masculinity and whiteness have been operationalized in society, we primarily focus on the differences between masculinity and whiteness experienced at the individual level. This individual analysis provides a practical entry point to explore identity interconnections between masculinity and whiteness.

Although no single aspect of identity exists in isolation, apart from other identities, it is important to note that individual experiences are greatly influenced by one's salient identities or those social identities that are most prominent across various contexts and situations (Jones & Abes, 2013). Generally, identity salience is determined by systemic contexts and the need to navigate those contexts. For example, race tends to be a common salient identity for People of Color because they have to navigate systemic racism in order to survive. Similarly, gender tends to be a salient identity for those who do not identify as men because these individuals must survive within the context of patriarchy. While identity salience does not negate the existence of dominant identities, like masculinity or whiteness, the intersection of salient oppressed identities shapes how dominant identities are experienced. Thus, the differences between masculinity and whiteness are largely observed through the lens of an individual's salient identities.

For those who identify as White men, the differences between masculinity and whiteness may not be understood because these individuals are typically unaware of their dominant identities and the systems of patriarchy and White supremacy. For those who hold at least one dominant identity, either masculinity or whiteness, and also a corresponding oppressed identity (e.g., Men of Color or White women), differences between masculinity and whiteness are largely shaped by identity salience. For example, Men of Color's understanding of what it means to be a man is largely impacted by the prevalence of racism (Harper, 2004). While these men certainly experience power and privilege as a result of their gender identity, the lived experience of that privilege is often filtered through the painful reality that Men of Color are socially targeted as threatening and dangerous within the context of White supremacy, often resulting in violence, brutality, and death. Conversely, White women's understanding of whiteness is significantly influenced by the context of patriarchy (Linder, 2016). Undoubtedly, these women benefit from White privilege, but those unearned advantages are often experienced in conjunction with the harsh daily implications of sexism, including misogyny, objectification, and sexual violence. Although Men of Color and White women are not the only ones who experience the differences between masculinity and whiteness, these two populations serve as illustrative examples of how identity salience often sheds light on the differences between masculinity and whiteness.

The differences between masculinity and whiteness tend to be most prevalent at the individual level and best understood within the context of corresponding salient identities. Neither masculinity nor whiteness exists in a vacuum, and salient intersecting identities have a profound impact on how these dominant identities are understood. An exploration of the identity interconnection between masculinity and whiteness must first grapple with the differences between these two identities to acknowledge multiple intersecting salient identities and their influence on how dominant identities are experienced at the individual level. Such an acknowledgment can then serve as a point of entry for exploring identity interconnections between masculinity and whiteness as a tool for developing critical consciousness and inspiring social justice action among individuals with dominant identities.

Commonalities Between Masculinity and Whiteness

An analysis of masculinity and whiteness reveals significant commonalities between these identities at the systemic level. While masculinity and whiteness manifest themselves differently at the individual level based on intersecting salient identities, these differences are often eclipsed by the presence of power associated with these identities within patriarchy and White supremacy.

Drawing from Kimmel's (2008) *Three Cultures of Guyland* and Frankenberg's (1993) *Three-Part Definition of Whiteness*, masculinity and whiteness can be understood as distinct social identities situated within a larger systemic context. Power and privilege are the common threads that connect patriarchy and White supremacy (Johnson, 2018). With this in mind, we have identified 10 commonalities between masculinity and whiteness at the systemic level. While this is not an exhaustive list, it does begin to demonstrate the commonalities of power and privilege between masculinity and whiteness. The 10 commonalities include the following:

- Masculinity and whiteness are both seen as the norm in U.S. society.
- Masculinity and whiteness both provide unearned benefits for the dominant group(s).
- Masculinity and whiteness both operate at the individual, interpersonal, and systemic levels.
- Masculinity and whiteness both persist through policies, patterns, and practices in culture and society, ensuring power for the dominant group(s).
- Masculinity and whiteness are both socially constructed manifestations of power but are believed to be natural and ordinary by those who hold dominance.
- Masculinity and whiteness are both tools of colonization, oppressively occupying the thoughts, emotions, and behaviors of those who are oppressed and those who hold dominant identities within those systems.
- Masculinity and whiteness both limit agency and individual freedoms of expression through the enforcement of policing and violence.
- Masculinity and whiteness both promote false mythologies of individualism and meritocracy.
- Masculinity and whiteness both persuade those with dominance to believe they are disconnected from others and not a part of systemic oppression.
- Masculinity and whiteness both dehumanize those who are oppressed and those who hold dominant identities albeit in distinct ways.

In concert with a systems-level exploration of commonalities between patriarchy and White supremacy, the analysis of differences on the individual level provides educators with a framework for using identity interconnections between masculinity and whiteness as a tool to develop critical consciousness and inspire social justice action among individuals with dominant identities.

Developing Critical Consciousness

When embarking on writing this chapter, we began by reflecting on our personal experiences with identity interconnections between masculinity and whiteness and discovered strong similarities between our stories. Specifically, we both testified to the influence that these identity interconnections had in developing our *critical consciousness* to the interconnected nature of inherited systems of power, resulting in a commitment to take action for social justice. Based on our own experiences, we define critical consciousness as the ability to reflect on one's salient identities and experiences within the context of interconnected systems in order to inform action for social justice. Given the individual differences and systemic commonalities between masculinity and whiteness, we believe that identity interconnections can be a powerful tool to develop critical consciousness and inspire social justice action among individuals with dominant identities.

We each began developing our critical consciousness as graduate students in student affairs master's programs. Having been raised in U.S. Midwest communities that largely upheld patriarchy and White supremacy, neither of us meaningfully reflected on our dominant social identities until we were in college, and even then, we resisted the reality of our own power and privilege as White men. Despite overwhelming evidence, we believed that we were somehow different from other White men, who we saw as solely responsible for sexism and racism. Instead of acknowledging our own role in patriarchy and White supremacy, we often focused on our individual good intentions when engaging in conversations about privilege. As we moved into graduate school, we experienced cognitive and emotional dissonance when fostering genuine relationships with peers who identified as women and People of Color. These relationships forced us to (re)examine our sexist and racist socialized beliefs and consider the possibility that we played a part in perpetuating inherited systems of power.

In fostering relationships with women and People of Color in graduate school, we initially reacted with emotional fragility, including intense feelings of guilt and shame that arose when discussing our privilege (DiAngelo, 2011; Linder, 2015). Rather than becoming more entrenched in our defensiveness, however, we began to develop critical consciousness. Further reflection on the experiences of women and People of Color, coupled with an exploration of critical scholarship related to masculinity and whiteness, allowed us to work through the cognitive and emotional dissonance associated with their fragility. Moreover, we realized that their experiences as White men were indeed shaped by patriarchy and White supremacy. Because of our common early life experiences related to transgressing and resisting traditional patriarchal masculinity, gender became a natural entry point for us to begin situating our personal experiences within inherited systems of power. As we reflected on our privilege in graduate school, our critical consciousness began developing, but only in relation to patriarchy. It was not until we understood identity interconnections between masculinity and whiteness that we began to see patriarchy and White supremacy as interconnected inherited systems of power.

For Brandon, identity interconnections between masculinity and whiteness came when he was introduced to Kimberlé Crenshaw's (1991) theory of intersectionality, which explains experiences of erasure for those who hold multiple intersecting oppressed identities (e.g., Women of Color) within inherited systems of power. Applying intersectionality to his knowledge about masculinity and patriarchy, Brandon began to consider how whiteness operates similarly within White supremacy by privileging White people and oppressing People of Color. For Kyle, identity interconnections between masculinity and whiteness were made when he attended the Social Justice Training Institute (SJTI), a weeklong intensive professional development opportunity for educators focused on racial justice. Having previously explored male privilege and patriarchy through his involvement in professional masculinity dialogue groups, he began to draw parallels between masculinity and whiteness as he grappled with his White privilege and the reality of White supremacy at SJTI.

Building off of our previously established understanding of power and privilege related to masculinity, we were able to turn our gaze inward, toward another dominant aspect of our identity, namely our whiteness. Through this process, we began to make connections and find commonalities across and between our privileged identities. Although we understood that the two identities were not the same, resulting in distinctly different forms of oppression for women and People of Color respectively, we came to see how patriarchy and White supremacy operated similarly at the systemic level. Through further reflection, we discovered that not only do patriarchy and White supremacy operate in similar ways, but they also mutually reinforce one another through systemic policies, institutional procedures, and cultural practices. This realization of interconnectivity enabled us to consider their own positionality within these interlocking inherited systems of power, resulting in a feeling of personal responsibility to take action for gender equity, racial justice, and social justice more broadly.

Indeed, observing identity interconnections between masculinity and whiteness enabled us to realize that neither gender equity nor racial justice would be achievable without holistic social justice action across all inherited systems of power. For example, striving for gender equity alone, without acknowledging interconnections between masculinity and whiteness, would not fully address the oppression experienced by Women of Color. Similarly, striving only for racial justice would not adequately disrupt the systems that oppress Women of Color and others who are marginalized by patriarchy. Identity interconnections between masculinity and whiteness can inspire individuals with dominant identities to take social justice action across all inherited systems of power because they reveal how systems are interconnected and mutually reinforcing. Furthermore, identity interconnections between masculinity and whiteness demonstrate how efforts across all inherited systems of power are necessary for social justice.

Practical Possibilities for Student Affairs Educators

Our experiences indicate that identity interconnections between masculinity and whiteness may hold practical possibilities for student affairs educators who aim to develop critical consciousness and inspire social justice action among individuals who hold dominant identities. Using identity interconnections between masculinity and whiteness, student affairs educators can help individuals who hold dominant identities critically examine those identities and situate them within interconnected systems of power to develop critical consciousness and inspire social justice action across all inherited systems of power. To illustrate the practical possibilities of this pedagogical tool, we explore three example scenarios where identity interconnections between masculinity and whiteness might be used to develop critical consciousness and inspire social justice action among individuals with dominant identities.

Engaging White Men Through Identity Interconnections

Consider a master's-level graduate student who identifies as a White man and is enrolled in a course that explores diversity and social justice topics. Coming from a privileged background, this student has likely not been challenged to think critically about any of his social identities before beginning graduate school, let alone consider the implications of power and privilege at the systemic level. As he becomes more immersed in his graduate school experience, he encounters perspectives, experiences, scholarship, and stories that challenge the hegemonic socialization of his early life. These critical incidents will likely result in cognitive and emotional dissonance for the student and trigger a reaction of emotional fragility intended to maintain his socialized assumptions of privilege and entitlement (DiAngelo, 2011).

As individuals with dominant identities begin exploring their privilege within inherited systems of power, it is typical for them to react with emotional fragility (Cabrera, 2012; DiAngelo, 2011). Just as we did when we began grappling with our privilege in graduate school, a common defensive maneuver for White men in these moments of cognitive and emotional dissonance is to retreat to the familiarity and comfort of their socialized position of dominance. When confronted with the disturbing possibility that they may be implicated in—and even responsible for—the oppression of others, individuals who identify as White men may attempt to defend themselves by articulating examples from their individual experience that demonstrate good intentions or personal innocence, thus excusing themselves from taking action for social justice (Cabrera, 2012).

By exploring identity interconnections between masculinity and whiteness, individuals who identify as White men can more easily shift their perspective from focusing solely on individual experiences to situating those experiences within larger inherited systems of power. Rather than narrowing their scope in an attempt to exonerate themselves in the face of systemic privilege, student affairs educators can use identity interconnections as a pedagogical tool to help individuals with dominant identities zoom out and consider how their multiple intersecting identities fit within the context of interconnected systems of power. Specifically, student affairs educators can compare and contrast patriarchy and White supremacy to demonstrate how inherited systems of power result in similar outcomes of power, privilege, and oppression.

Student affairs educators can engage individuals who identify as White men in the development of critical consciousness and inspire them to take action for social justice by using identity interconnections between masculinity and whiteness. One way to do this may involve reviewing McIntosh's (1988) *Privilege Knapsack* with individuals and then asking them to identify similar examples of privilege related to other dominant identities, like masculinity. Another way student affairs educators might use identity inter-connections between masculinity and whiteness with individuals who iden-tify as White men would be to create opportunities for them to reflect on their implicit biases by taking the Implicit Association Tests related to gender and race (Greenwald et al., 1998). Afterward, educators can invite students to reflect on their results and consider the differences and commonalities between biases related to masculinity and whiteness.

Engaging White Women Through Identity Interconnections

Imagine a new student affairs professional who identifies as a White woman and is heavily involved in feminist activism on campus. She serves as a pro-gram coordinator for the Women's Center and was charged with organizing a series of Sexual Assault Awareness Month events. Through past conversa-tions, it is clear that gender equity and feminism are very important to her, and she spends a significant amount of time advocating for victim-survivors of sexual assault on campus. Although she has an understanding of racism broadly, she struggles to apply an interconnected approach to her feminist efforts. Specifically, this new professional has resisted opportunities provided by Women of Color for her to reflect on her White privilege and how her whiteness has caused her to prioritize White women in her feminist efforts.

Student affairs educators can engage colleagues (and students) like the one described previously by applying identity interconnections between masculin-ity and whiteness to develop critical consciousness. While having experience with the oppression caused by patriarchy, this student affairs professional does not have critical consciousness about White supremacy as an inherited system of power. Given that gender is a salient identity for her, and race is not, her understanding of whiteness is primarily filtered through her perspective as a woman. Students who identify as White women may prefer to focus on addressing patriarchy, while remaining unaware of and resistant to addressing their role in perpetuating White supremacy. Rather than allowing this col-league to pivot away from the dissonance caused by situating her racial identity within the context of White supremacy, student affairs educators can employ identity interconnections between masculinity and whiteness to engage her and others who identify as White women in developing critical consciousness.

Engaging this individual in an exploration of the commonalities and differences between masculinity and whiteness may provide a pathway to critical consciousness and inspire her to take social justice action. To do this, student affairs educators might encourage individuals who identify as White women to facilitate a campus program related to the historical role of allies within feminist and racial justice movements. Then, the educators can invite individuals to reflect on the commonalities and differences between these movements, as well as the need for women and People of Color to form social justice coalitions. Alternatively, student affairs educators can encourage individuals who identify as White women to foster meaningful and authentic relationships with People of Color and consider how women can support antiracism efforts on campus. Through this process, student affairs educators can invite individuals who identify as White women to reflect on how they might honor the voices of People of Color in feminist movements and contribute to campus racial justice efforts.

Engaging Men of Color Through Identity Interconnections
Bring to mind a senior student affairs officer who identifies as a Latinx man. The founder of a Latinx professional affinity group on campus and an advisor to a Latino Greek-letter organization, this individual has a strong commitment to racial justice for Students of Color at his institution. Despite having a thorough understanding of how racism and White privilege result from White supremacy, this professional often fails to acknowledge the unearned privileges he receives as a man and the impact of sexism on those who do not identify as men within the system of patriarchy. Specifically, this individual has resisted feedback from Women of Color colleagues who tried to hold him accountable after making dismissive comments toward the women in his department.

By applying identity interconnections between masculinity and whiteness, student affairs educators can engage this individual in developing his critical consciousness and inspire him to take action for social justice. While having experience with the oppression caused by White supremacy, this professional does not fully understand patriarchy as an inherited system of power. Given that race is a salient identity for this individual, and gender is not, his understanding of masculinity is primarily filtered through his perspective as a Person of Color. Individuals who identify as Men of Color may prefer to focus on addressing White supremacy while remaining unaware of and resistant to addressing their role in perpetuating patriarchy. Rather than allowing these men to pivot away from the dissonance caused by situating their gender within the context of patriarchy, educators can engage individuals who identify as Men of Color in developing critical consciousness and inspire them to take social justice action by using identity interconnections between masculinity and whiteness.

To do this, student affairs educators may consider encouraging the individual to attend a campus event hosted by the Women's Center focused on engaging men in feminist efforts and then having a reflective conversation about the commonalities and differences between patriarchy and White supremacy. Alternatively, student affairs educators might encourage Men of Color to volunteer with local organizations that support women's health and then reflect on how People of Color can contribute to feminist efforts. Engaging these individuals in an exploration of identity interconnections between masculinity and whiteness may provide a pathway to developing critical consciousness and taking social justice action.

Scholarly and Practical Considerations

Some student affairs scholars and educators might be curious the possibilities of applying identity interconnections to dominant identities that are not discussed in this chapter. This line of inquiry might include questions like, do identity interconnections between heterosexuality and whiteness hold the same possibilities for developing critical consciousness and inspiring social justice action among individuals who identify as heterosexual and/or White? Could an educator effectively utilize identity interconnections between able-bodiedness and masculinity to develop critical consciousness and inspire social justice action with individuals about ableism and patriarchy? While we believe that identity interconnections between other dominant identities would likely be effective in developing critical consciousness and inspiring social justice action, we cannot say with certainty that these tools would have the same impact as the one discussed in this chapter. Claims about the practical possibilities of other identity interconnections are beyond the scope of this chapter. In order to better understand the practical possibilities of identity interconnections across and between other areas of dominance, scholars must take up the task of investigating the implications of such an approach.

Additionally, some student affairs educators may wonder if identity interconnections between masculinity and whiteness might be effective in developing critical consciousness and inspiring social justice action among undergraduate college students. Given that we encountered identity interconnections between masculinity and whiteness during and beyond graduate school, we cannot say with certainty that this tool would have the same impact on undergraduate students as it did for us. That said, we have professional and anecdotal evidence to suggest that undergraduate students are now entering college with increasingly greater critical consciousness about inherited systems of power than ever before. If this is true, identity interconnections may be an incredibly timely and appropriate pedagogical tool for fostering that critical consciousness and inspiring social justice action among undergraduate students.

Student affairs educators and scholars who use identity interconnections between masculinity and whiteness must engage in compassionate caution when considering how to be good stewards of this tool (Duran et al., 2019). One of the best ways to ensure that identity interconnections between masculinity and whiteness are being used appropriately and meaningfully is for student affairs educators who employ the tool to engage in an ongoing praxis of developing critical consciousness and taking social justice action in their own lives. Modeling this development is crucial because it allows student affairs educators to more effectively invite individuals with dominant identities into developing critical consciousness and taking social justice action, while reducing the possibility of resistance. By demonstrating how to develop critical consciousness and taking social justice action, student affairs educators can model how individuals with dominant identities can use identity interconnections between masculinity and whiteness as a pathway into understanding and supporting those who are oppressed. Finally, student affairs educators should model how individuals with dominant identities might use identity interconnections between masculinity and whiteness to effectively foster social justice coalitions across and between different identities.

CONCLUSION

Over thirty years ago, Peggy McIntosh (1988) published *The Privilege Knapsack*. Since that time, this landmark document has been used to start conversations about White privilege around the globe. Despite the monumental significance of her work, few educators in the field of student affairs in higher education discuss identity interconnections between masculinity, whiteness, and their associated systems of power, which McIntosh compared to better understand her own White privilege. Other critical and poststructural theorists have similarly demonstrated the interlocking nature of systems of power, namely the mutually reinforcing dynamics that work to uphold racism, sexism, classism, and heterosexism, to name a few (Collins, 2004; Crenshaw, 1991; hooks, 2004; Lorde, 1985; Tatum, 1997).

This chapter attempts to build upon the legacy of McIntosh and vision-ary Women of Color scholars by exploring identity interconnections between masculinity and whiteness. While experienced differently, mas-culinity and whiteness have striking commonalities at the systemic level. As a result of our own personal experience with identity interconnections between masculinity and whiteness, we developed critical consciousness, or the ability to reflect on one's salient identities and experiences within the context of interconnected systems of power to inform action for social justice. Additionally, we came to realize the need for holistic social justice action across all inherited systems of power. These realizations, along with critical scholarship related to patriarchy and White supremacy, demonstrate practical possibilities for student affairs educators to use identity intercon-nections between masculinity and whiteness as a pedagogical tool to develop critical consciousness and inspire social justice action among individuals who hold dominant identities.

REFERENCES

Cabrera, N. L. (2012). Working through Whiteness: White, male college students challenging racism. *The Review of Higher Education, 35*(3), 375–401. https://doi .org/10.1353/rhe.2012.0020

Collins, P. H. (2004). Toward a new vision: Race, class, and gender as categories of analysis and connection. In L. Heldke & P. O'Connor (Eds.), *Oppression, privi-lege, and resistance* (pp. 529–543). McGraw-Hill.

Crenshaw, K. (1991). Mapping the margins: Intersectionality, identity politics, and violence against women of color. *Stanford Law Review, 43*, 1241–1299. https:// doi.org/10.2307/1229039

DiAngelo, R. (2011). White fragility. *International Journal of Critical Pedagogy, 3*(3), 54–70. https://libjournal.uncg.edu/ijcp/article/view/249

Duran, A., Pope, R. L., & Jones, S. R. (2019). The necessity of intersectionality as a framework to explore queer and trans student retention. *Journal of College Student Retention: Research, Theory, and Practice, 21*(4), 520–543. https://doi .org/10.1177/1521025119895510

Frankenberg, R. (1993). Growing up White: Feminism, racism, and the social geography of childhood. *Thinking Through Ethnicities*, (45), 51–84. https://doi .org/10.2307/1395347

Greenwald, A. G., McGhee, D. E., & Schwartz, J. L. K. (1998). Measuring individual differences in implicit cognition: The Implicit Association Test. *Journal of Personality*

and Social Psychology, 74(6), 1464–1480. https://doi.org/10.1037//0022-3514
.74.6.1464

Harper, S. R. (2004). The measure of a man: Conceptualizations of masculinity
among high-achieving African American male college students. *Berkeley Journal
of Sociology, 48*(1), 89–107. https://www.jstor.org/stable/41035594

hooks, b. (2004). *The will to change: Men, masculinity, and love.* Washington Square
Press.

Johnson, A. (2001). *Privilege, power, & difference.* Mayfield.

Jones, S. R., & Abes, E. S. (2013). *Identity development of college students: Advancing
frameworks for multiple dimensions of identity.* Jossey-Bass.

Keating, A. (2013). *Transformation now! Toward a post oppositional politics of change.*
University of Illinois Press.

Kimmel, M. (2008). *Guyland: The perilous world where boys become men.* Harper.

Koch, K. (2012, December 19). Using privilege helpfully. *The Harvard Gazette.*
https://news.harvard.edu/gazette/story/2012/12/using-privilege-helpfully/

Lensmire, T. J., McManimon, S. K., Dockter Tierney, J., Lee-Nichols, M. E., Casey,
Z. A., Lensmire, A., & Davis, B. M. (2013). McIntosh as synecdoche: How teacher
education's focus on White privilege undermines antiracism. *Harvard Educational
Review, 83*(3), 410–432. https://doi.org/10.17763/haer.83.3.35054h14l8230574

Linder, C. (2015). Navigating guilt, shame, and fear of appearing racist: A conceptual model of antiracist White feminist identity development. *Journal of College
Student Development, 56*(6), 535–550. https://doi.org/10.1353/csd.2015.0057

Lorde, A. (1985). *Sister outsider.* Crossing Press.

McIntosh, P. (1988). White privilege: Unpacking the invisible knapsack. In *White
privilege and male privilege: A personal account of coming to see correspondences
through work in women's studies* (Working Paper 189). Wellesley College Center
for Research on Women.

McIntosh, P. (2008). White privilege: Unpacking the invisible knapsack. In
P. Rothenberg (Ed.), *White privilege: Essential readings on the other side of racism*
(pp. 123–127). Worth.

Moraga, C., & Anzaldúa, G. (Eds.). (2015). *This bridge called my back: Writings by
radical women of color* (4th ed.). State University of New York Press.

Tatum, B. (1997). *"Why are all the Black kids sitting together in the cafeteria?" and
other conversations about race.* Basic Books.

9

Identity Interconnections, Coalitions, and Possibilities

Lessons from the Creation of an Asian Pacific Islander Middle Eastern Desi American Service Office

Windi N. Sasaki

I N 2014, STUDENTS AT the University of California, San Diego published an open letter demanding, among other things, an "Asian Pacific Islander Middle Eastern Desi American Research and Resource Center (APIMEDA RRC)" (Coalition for Critical Asian American Studies [CCAAS], 2014, para. 6). They wanted a space on campus for APIMEDA students—whom the campus does not include in their definition of under-served populations (University of California [UC] at San Diego Student Retention Services, n.d.), but whom students believe need community, retention, leadership, and academic services to be successful. The students felt that their experiences with microaggressions, invisibility, and racism were similar across Asian American, Pacific Islander, Middle Eastern, and Desi American communities. About 2 years later, I was hired as the APIMEDA program manager and tasked with determining how best to serve these populations.

This chapter provides an example of the application of identity interconnections to the process of developing a student services office. Building an office as the APIMEDA program manager has meant balancing the perceived and actual experiences of APIMEDA students and the people who interact with APIMEDA students. Weaving together Keating's (2013) lessons for interconnectivity and Watt's (2015) engaging difference to develop coalitions that create change, I describe the efforts to build an office that seeks to acknowledge the shared aspects of these students' experiences and address the distinct needs of diverse APIMEDA populations on a college campus.

THEORETICAL FRAMEWORK

Keating's (2013) observations and reflections on creating successful coalition relationships provide a template for how listening to and understanding the similarities and differences between groups seeking to be in coalition is instrumental to their success. In viewing APIMEDA students as a coalition of peoples, seeing the interconnections is an integral part of developing a new office supporting these communities. In addition, Watt's (2015) Authentic, Action-oriented Framing for Environmental Shifts (AAFES) provides guidance for higher education to ask questions, build relationships, and operationalize ideas for creating lasting change. Similar to Keating, Watt describes listening and the authentic desire to create a new environment or initiative as an assumption in actions that lead to creating lasting change. These transformational environments demonstrate a new collective reality rather than retrofitting existing realities to the people one seeks to serve. Throughout this chapter, I describe student activism and coalition building, analyze that activism using Keating's and Watt's ideas, explore how that analysis informs a way forward, and reflect on how those events continue the cycle of listening, building relationships, and moving forward to support diverse student populations.

THE EXPERIENCES OF THE CCAAS STUDENTS

Located in the southern- and westernmost county in California, UC San Diego is a large, public university, with over 30,000 undergraduate and 7,000 graduate and professional students. As of fall 2020, students who apply to any campus of the University of California system have nearly 70 race and ethnicity options that they can choose from on an optional demographic survey. Of those options, 15 are Asian and Desi ethnicities, six are Pacific Islander ethnicities, and 32 are Southwest Asian and North African (SWANA) ethnicities. Of those 54, four are "other" so that applicants can select an option in their racial group even when their ethnicity is not listed. According to the UC Information Center (n.d.a) disaggregated data chart, in fall 2020, approximately 38% of the undergraduate population at UC San Diego was Asian American, 0.7% were Pacific Islander, and 5.4% were SWANA American. The chart also provides a full disaggregation by reported ethnicities of all undergraduate students and domestic graduate students.

When the student group, CCAAS, wrote their demands in 2014, they were responding to their own experiences and experiences of microaggressions that were reported at other Southern California universities. These incidents were most commonly shared or discovered on social media, with students from those campuses often seeking support and solidarity from students in CCAAS and other UC San Diego Asian American student organizations. UC San Diego students believed they faced similar microaggressions related to the model minority stereotype (the suggestion that Asian American people are all hardworking overachievers; Chang 2011), the perpetual foreigner stereotype (the suggestion that all Asian American people are foreign and incapable of assimilation into American culture; Kim, 1999), Islamophobia (the overgeneralization that people who are Muslim are connected to terrorism, resulting in misinformation and inhospitable environments; Ahmadi & Cole, 2020), and other harmful stereotypes. In addition, the students saw a decrease in the availability of classes related to Asian American and Pacific Islander peoples and histories as there were few faculty able to teach these classes. When students sought psychological counseling, they found that there was only one permanent Asian American counselor in the department, and that person had an administrative appointment that limited his availability to see clients. During their meetings with and presentations to administrators and other staff and faculty, students shared stories of difficulties finding culturally relevant mentors and staff on campus.

The CCAAS students understood that the campus population of APIMEDA students is made up of dozens of populations. Within each population are people with a large diversity of cultural practices, ancestral languages spoken, migration histories, religions practiced, and other things that might be mistakenly assumed as common for people across a racial category. The students, most of whom identified as Asian American, shared their specific ethnic identities and recounted experiences of being assumed to be from another ethnic population or told that only their racial identity mattered to people with whom they interacted on campus. Because the Asian American population on campus was perceived as large, students were often told that they had privilege. The students objected; they did not see themselves reflected in the services, coursework, staff, or faculty as their White peers did. They described stories where this was amplified for first-generation college students, low-income students, and children of refugees. They believed that these experiences were likely similar for their Pacific Islander peers.

Within CCAAS was an Arab American student (who uses they series pronouns). The Arab American student connected with the group of Asian American students because they observed similarities in experiences to their own. As an Arab American, they felt they were expected to identify as White on demographic surveys, since the United States includes Middle Eastern people in the "White" racial category on the Census (Wiltz, 2014). The Arab American student objected to this, as they did not have the same experiences as their European White peers. They had experienced microaggressions related to their Arab American identity and other assumed identities. When they heard Asian American students talk about their experiences, they found a place to connect. When this student joined CCAAS, they became an integral part of the advocacy. When the students finalized their open letter, the group shared that it had become important to include Middle Eastern American people. The students had seen the ways that their experiences overlapped and the ways that all of their communities would benefit from the types of support they were advocating for.

The acronym APIMEDA came to CCAAS after a long meeting trying to create a descriptor for the emerging coalition. They acknowledged that any name they created would be imperfect. They also knew that the name needed to resonate with the students whom they wanted to feel seen and served by the campus. For the student leaders, their collective advocacy unified a coalition of interconnected communites similar to how the term *Asian American* was coined in the 1960s by Emma Gee and Yuji Ichioka at UC Berkeley (Kambhampaty, 2020)—a term for students advocating for their collective needs despite their ethnic differences and unique experiences on campus.

The students' open letter (CCAAS, 2014) included 11 named demands, including an increase in Asian American and Pacific Islander faculty and staff hiring and an expansion of coursework and services related to APIMEDA populations, and to the publishing of transparent and disaggregated data related to APIMEDA students. The letter included a specific ask for an APIMEDA Research and Resource Center; a dedicated space for students would be able to visit with faculty teaching courses on APIMEDA peoples, attend special lectures, and engage in research. While in the physical space working with faculty, students envisioned dedicated staff would work on retention efforts, such as creating events to encourage a sense of community, develop leadership skills, and provide career development for APIMEDA communities. The students hoped for a space that would be a hub of activities for every part of their life on campus.

UNDERSTANDING THE IDENTITY INTERCONNECTIONS OF APIMEDA STUDENTS

The way that the members of CCAAS and their allies talked about advocacy acknowledged similar experiences between APIMEDA students and differences that APIMEDA students experience based on their different identities. Student discussions to identify common needs included examining where their experiences were different as opportunities to explore aspiring allyship between APIMEDA communities. As Keating (2013) describes, this discussion provided them with a rich base to examine needs, build strong connections, and seek greater support across identities.

Similarities Across APIMEDA Student Populations

When students spoke of their similarities, the narratives tended to surround their experiences with invisibility and their experiences with microaggressions and macroaggressions. Students shared stories of feeling invisible on campus. They could not find faculty or staff who identified similarly to them, and there were a few courses on their histories and stories. When they saw campus data reported, they often did not see themselves represented, in part because Asian American undergraduate students are often reported in the same race category as Asian international undergraduate students. In fall 2019, international students made up 17.6% of the undergraduate student population (UC San Diego, Office of Institutional Research, n.d.), with the largest portion, over two thirds, from China (UC Information Center, n.d.b). Asian American students believed aggregated reporting blurred their experiences and histories in the United States with Asian international students and reinforced perpetual foreigner stereotypes. In addition, they believed that the aggregated data did not illuminate the diversity of the population or differences within the Asian American population.

For example, according to their 2015 report, The Campaign for College Opportunity found that some of the smallest populations of Southeast Asian American people in the state of California had the lowest rates of access to and graduation from every level of the public higher education system. When these concerns were brought up, the members of CCAAS were told that the Asian population in aggregate was large and so these things were not a concern. This reinforced feelings of invisibility for some populations within the Asian American aggregated demographic. The Pacific Islander populations were often left out of charts or not discussed at all. It was assumed that their experiences were the same as their Asian and Asian American peers. This idea has been widely disputed (Empowering Pacific Islander Communities & Asian Americans Advancing Justice, 2014; The Campaign for College Opportunity, 2015) and does not serve the Pacific Islander community. SWANA American students began reporting their ethnicity information on the UC application, starting with the class entering fall 2014 (UC Office of Equity, Diversity, and Inclusion, n.d.). Despite collecting this information, there are few places where students can find this data represented. In 2020, SWANA American people had their data collected and reported as "White" to federal agencies, including the Census, Department of Education, and Department of Justice (Wiltz, 2014). Many SWANA American students shared that they did not identify as White, nor are they typically perceived as White by other people.

Students also shared common experiences with microaggressions and macroaggressions. Students from all ethnic populations were assumed to be international students or foreign-born. People made comments assuming their ethnic identity, religion, majors, study schedules, and interests. These were through social media posts, flyers posted on campus, comments made in classrooms, residences, or other places where students gathered, and in response to their demands. Students who understood these experiences as similar, even when the content or the target was different, tended to participate in coalition spaces more than students who did not. They shared their experiences of invisibility, microaggressions, and macroaggressions with one another, and engaged one another with empathy. These similar experiences provided a place to develop relationships to form coalitions and shared learning.

Differences Across APIMEDA Student Populations

Despite these similar experiences, students were aware that there are differences in their experiences. The relative sizes of the populations varied largely, from as few as one student to as many as 4,000 students. Migration patterns of various groups are also different, as some Pacific Islander populations are indigenous to the United States and its territories. The rest of the APIMEDA population shared that they are between first generation and eighth generation in the United States. In addition, histories of conflicts in other parts of the world have caused division between some ethnic populations as those conflicts elsewhere have affected students' families.

Even within ethnic populations, students may speak different languages, be multiethnic or multiracial, practice different religions, and come from different class backgrounds. Students have different experiences with their own identity developments because there may be differences in the salience of their ethnic identities. For some, their ethnic identity may be mediated by another identity, such as their gender identity, sexual orientation, generation, or religion.

While noticing similarities has provided students with a space to develop coalitions, differences often stop students from developing these relationships. There has sometimes been a complicated history between populations that exist within and between groups. And, because of the many ways students mistaken for another ethnicity, there may be resistance to joining a coalitional group if it isn't clear that the intragroup differences are understood. In the ways that Keating (2013) describes listening with raw openness as difficult, some members of the campus communities have found it difficult to remain engaged and persist through the complicated narratives and stories of each of the different perspectives within APIMEDA communities. However, when students make the decision that their similarities are an important reason to keep listening, they have been able to build strong relationships and coalitions with one another.

CREATING APIMEDA PROGRAMS AND SERVICES

When I was hired in 2016, I started with listening. I reached out to our alumni who had been involved in CCAAS, reached out to as many APIMEDA-related student organizations that would agree to meet with me, created a survey for students to take, and reviewed how other campuses served portions of the population I was tasked with serving. After considering what I learned and information shared by CCAAS members during their activism, it became clear that the formation of APIMEDA Programs and Services needed to address the following:

- CCAAS (2014) provided their demands as an attempt to bridge the gaps—whether in understanding, resource needs, transition to and from college, or connecting students to the campus community. How would my position create an opportunity to forge a new, transformational space in those gaps?
- How could I talk about the commonalities in migration, values, culture, and oppression between the groups included in this program and its spaces in ways that would resonate with all ethnic populations included in the APIMEDA communities, and challenge the assumptions that many stakeholders have of who APIMEDA people are?
- How could I create a transformational space that supports the needs of the coalition while acknowledging and including the broad diversity present within APIMEDA communities?
- Where would it be important to discern and distinguish between diverse ethnic populations? This discussion was particularly important so that students understood their inclusion within the construction of the APIMEDA coalition.

Framed by understanding the naming conventions within the APIMEDA construct and drawing from Espiritu's (1992) descriptions of panethnicity and transformative spaces, these questions provided a framework for me to communicate with others about how to construct the community. Consistent with Keating's (2013) ideas of interconnectivity, it was clear that the office needed to be formed so that people could see themselves and their experiences reflected without flattening their narratives and experiences as the same. The students did not see themselves as having the same experiences, and a successful transformational space would need to affirm that they were not synonymous, while building and strengthening their bonds as a coalition of people navigating similar institutional barriers.

In meeting with students, I told them that we had the unique opportunity to create something new, something that could serve them well and include all of their identities. In encouraging their creativity, I hoped to forge new realities in our environment where students felt more seen and better served. In prioritizing this work to establish my office, I placed many of the initiatives into three groups: understanding APIMEDA as a coalition of peoples rather than a community, honoring individual community needs in balance with serving the entire APIMEDA student population, and encouraging the broader staff and faculty population on campus to learn more about APIMEDA students in ways that influence how we serve and support these populations.

Moving From Community to Coalition

When people are asked what comes to mind when they hear the word "community," they often describe ideas present in the definition of the word: people with shared interests or characteristics (Merriam Webster, n.d.). In contrast, the CCAAS (2014) Open Letter attributed community to a communal experience of wellness and visibility. Their demands and words tied more directly to a need for representation in all places within the university structure, including student services and the curriculum of the university. In calling for the disaggregation of admissions and retention data, students indicated that their advocacy was driven by an understanding of the interconnections of their experiences and asked for change in solidarity. This solidarity fueled a coalition, defined as a temporary alliance of distinct parties or persons for joint action (Merriam Webster, n.d.). However, the language that CCAAS used in their demands discussed community. My conversations with students who had not been connected to CCAAS's advocacy revealed they did not understand themselves as part of the same community with other APIMEDA people. It became clear that I needed to communicate differently to different students about how they could be included in the services my office provides.

I became more intentional about how I talk about whom I serve. I now explain APIMEDA as a coalition made up of several communities. These are subtle language choices intended to signal an understanding of the diversity within the APIMEDA coalition, such as the words used in the coalition's name, and within each of the ethnic populations included in the coalition's name. I intend to communicate that I understand the diversity of identities and experiences within all levels of the group, acknowledging that some narratives are different, and that while my role is to support the collective, I also understand that not everyone needs the same thing. This distinction has allowed the students with whom I interact to create their own relationships with the coalition, share their own stories, and be open to connecting with other groups with whom they have not previously seen a connection. What I see from the students and organizations connected with my office is a willingness to find ways to connect with others—they see opportunities to work with one another, collaborate, and learn from one another. As Keating (2013) shares, it is important for the members of the coalition to find connections based on their commonalities without denying their differences.

Outside of communication, coalition work has become the central idea behind providing student organization support and leadership education.

Student Organization Support

Previously, student organizations often did not realize when they talked about the same issues and thus missed opportunities to learn from one another or collaborate. This was about more than how the APIDA premedical student organization could work with the Filipinx American premedical student association. It would involve the Palestinian American organization connecting with the Pacific Islander organization to address colonization, or the Pan-Arab organization connecting with any of the Southeast Asian American organizations to have similar conversations about refugee experiences. In addition to suggesting that the student organizations connect, I needed to explain and offer background about where their conversations overlapped, where they likely didn't, and why it was important for them to join their efforts.

Leadership Education

When the students involved in the organizations affiliated with my office discuss why they are involved, they usually identify similar themes: students seeking to support their peers, a desire to make their communities stronger, and the hope of leaving the community and the campus better. Students express feeling personally responsible for the collective success of their communities, and I believe that this provides an opportunity for students to work in coalition and share this responsibility for their communities. Outside of individual and organization consultations, I started to host an APIMEDA Community and Coalition Conference. The conference is a shared group experience for the participants to expand how they might conceive of opportunities for coalition building and achieve change that outlasts their direct involvement in the activity. Central to the Conference is Sherry Watt's (2015) authentic, action-oriented framing for environmental shifts (AAFES) method. AAFES provides a framework for participants to reflect on their goals for change on campus or in their communities and explore what opportunities exist to bring in others to create change. AAFES requires individuals to consider how their own ideas have changed by listening to those who need to be involved in their efforts to make change. These ideas are similar to Keating's (2013) lessons of interconnectivity, used to create a new intervention and path forward. Participants have successfully reached out to connect with others, bringing in others who can sustain the efforts they started, and forge new partnerships.

Honoring Individual Community Needs While Serving APIMEDA Students Broadly

In my attempts to serve the population broadly, I have drawn upon common experiences and needs to describe what APIMEDA Programs and Services does. This is a necessity, as most students interact with my office initially through our website or a brief presentation at a large event. Finding the similarities provides a way in and is useful when discussing how students can successfully use campus resources, network with others, and build coalitions.

In bringing together APIMEDA peoples, I acknowledge that different populations have different experiences in their inclusion in any racial coalition. This has affected the way that each community has felt seen (or not) on campus. As much as I work with students to build coalitions, I know that it is important for them to find community in a way that will fulfill them. This has resulted in working with students to host affinity community lunches for smaller populations of APIMEDA students to help them connect. As a result, new organizations have formed that provide points of connection and community for students. Students have also asked about programming to educate the campus community about their experiences. My office partners with these groups to host films, lectures, performances, and other activities for community members. The APIMEDA office also regularly shares points of history about people and events from different APIMEDA communities on our social media and website. We have noticed these posts being shared widely within and outside of our campus community. This work increases the visibility of specific ethnic communities whom we are discussing and reiterates the important message that the coalition is diverse. It also encourages others to learn by providing multiple avenues to find a connection in their own narratives.

Responding to Staff and Faculty Understandings
of APIMEDA Students

In addition to meeting with students, it has been important to my work to establish connections with campus staff and faculty. In talking with these partners, I have learned what assumptions and generalizations they tend to make about these student communities. Most partners talked about APIMEDA students as though they are all Asian and Asian American students. Some staff and faculty have made assertions that align with model minority stereotypes. Others have shared that they perceive the entire population to be comprised of students who were not born in the United States. Most colleagues do not understand the diverse needs present in Asian American and APIMEDA communities. Few colleagues have been able to describe any of the issues facing Pacific Islander students, and all issues described for Middle Eastern American students only relate to Islamophobia, despite the religious diversity within this population. These conversations have illuminated an immediate need to better educate staff and faculty about APIMEDA students.

CCAAS (2014) described gaps in student services and feeling misunderstood on campus, underscoring the need for a network of campus partners to better understand working with APIMEDA students. My office only serves a portion of the students who identify as APIMEDA. In order for APIMEDA students to interact with staff and faculty who understand their experiences across campus, I created several interventions

Opportunities for Learning
Over the past few years, I have brought scholars in to discuss the complexities within various parts of APIMEDA populations. I have also hosted workshops and a summer reading group challenging existing practice, raising awareness about smaller subgroups of the APIMEDA student populations, and sharing resources where colleagues can learn more. My office's website also offers a plethora of resources and readings that I often refer people to when they want to learn more.

Encourage Question Asking
I often open presentations to campus partners with the list of 54 ethnicity options under Asian/Asian American, Pacific Islander, and Southwest Asian

and North African on the UC application for admission. On occasion, this is preceded by a request that people try to name as many of these ethnic populations as they can recall. I share that it is impossible for any one person to know everything about each one of these populations, even me. This means that there are opportunities for us all to learn. After admitting that we have places for learning, we can ask questions and investigate where we can take responsibility for learning how to answer our own questions. In addition, the newness of the display of any disaggregated data for our students allows for staff to recognize where there might be differences and similarities between groups. I ask that staff use these new and developing resources to analyze the information critically, ask questions, and take action to better serve our students.

Be Comfortable With Complexity

I am often asked, "What do APIMEDA students need?" There are many answers to this question. The answers are rarely the same for all populations and communities. Once I was able to get past my desire to give people a simple, satisfying answer to their question, I have needed to find ways to help others understand that they have asked a complex question with no singular answer. Most often, I share that students want to feel seen and represented and want to interact with people who understand their culture. This means those of us interacting with these students need to understand that the APIMEDA populations are a grouping of highly diverse communities and that there is no singular "APIMEDA culture." As Keating (2013) asserts, this requires us to take a step back, listen for understanding, and ask questions before moving to address the needs of the students immediately.

IMPLICATIONS FOR STUDENT AFFAIRS PRACTICE

It may be easy to read my examples within a multicultural affairs–specific context. However, I encourage student affairs colleagues in all parts of the field to consider how the practices and questions presented in this chapter are necessary and relevant for all functional areas and contexts that support student development. As ethnic populations diversify in the United States, all identity-based spaces on college campuses that are not talking about coalitions will likely need to move in that direction, no matter if they have a designated multicultural center or not. LGBT centers have been trying to do this for decades. And, in order to best serve and support these diverse students, everyone on the campus—no matter their role or functional area—needs to think of the implications of categories and coalitions. APIMEDA students interact with every part of the campus, not just offices like mine. The CCAAS students explained their needs of different offices. The request for an office or space like mine was about having at least one space where they felt welcomed and served. Our goal should be that students find these spaces everywhere they visit and live on campus.

Understanding Student Populations

In understanding the populations of students with whom we are working, it is important to discern when we see similarities that we can address collectively, and when acknowledging differences and the uniqueness between populations is necessary. The ways we communicate with students will indicate to them our understanding of their shared and unique experiences. Choosing words that do not assume their identities or experiences can provide a meaningful starting place. It is also important to be conscious of particular words that might have a bias toward one group or another, regardless of the intent. For example, there are times when I am only talking about our Pacific Islander students, and it would then be inappropriate for me to discuss them using the entire APIMEDA coalition name. There are also other inclusive language terms related to gender identity, ability, or other identifiers that can be strong indicators to student audiences that, at a minimum, student affairs educators are not erasing them or flattening their experiences to fit into a larger portion of the campus population.

The ways that student affairs offices report data can also indicate whether we have considered the diversity of the student communities with whom we work. Small racial populations, like Pacific Islander students and Native American students, are sometimes excluded from racial data. While their numbers may be small (and in some cases they may not be represented on campuses at all), it is all the more important to acknowledge and accurately state the names and sizes of these populations. Their omission from reported demographics data further marginalizes these communities and contributes to the lack of understanding that universities have of these populations (Shotton et al., 2013). In addition, some students may prefer to have their identity data displayed in ways similar to how they were asked to provide it, rather than have it reported in aggregate. At UC San

Diego, this has not only meant displaying data for Pacific Islander and Native American students separately, but also for SWANA American populations and students who identify as trans or nonbinary. Some students, as the CCAAS (2014) student leaders did in their open letter, have also felt affirmed when they see their specific ethnicity displayed in demographics data. I have interacted with several students who have expressed genuine excitement at learning that there are dozens of students who share their ethnicity on our campus. For some students, these numbers have made them feel less alone and hopeful that they might interact with a peer who identifies in a similar way to them.

When we expand our understanding of how students might identify, we challenge limited and limiting assumptions of community. This is particularly important at the intersections of identity. For example, because I work with SWANA American populations, different campus partners have assumed that I work with the Muslim community. While I do and have worked with Muslim students around some of their needs, it is also important that these identities (SWANA American students and Muslim students) are not conflated. While many of the students connected with the Muslim Student Association identify as South Asian American or SWANA American, Black and Southeast Asian American students also actively participate in the Muslim Student Association's activities. My campus partners in the Black Resource Center and other centers provide support to students using their spaces, and we work collectively to provide advocacy. In addition, not all of our SWANA American students are Muslim, which is often assumed to be the case. The experiences of Muslim and SWANA American students may also be different based on students' gender identity, sexual orientation, class, and generation status in the United States. By not conflating the ethnic or religious identities of our students, we can be more effective inviting students with diverse intersecting identities in and building connections across departments to better advocate for these students.

Coalition Versus Community

As I explained previously, using coalition language to talk about the large group of students with whom I work has led to more students understanding their connections to other groups of students. It has also allowed me to find ways to expand campus colleagues' ideas of connection and create innovative opportunities and partnerships. In talking with students,

I have found that it is important to evaluate and clarify if the people being served are a community or a coalition, and which language will best serve the population. This often starts with listening for understanding to the experiences of students.

If student affairs educators determine that coalition language is most appropriate, it is essential to explain this connection is based on similarities, not sameness. This attentiveness to engaging identity interconnections with compassionate caution provides an opportunity for others to see why and how they might connect and listen to one another. When engaging students, I explain that these skills (of listening with raw openness and pursuing radical interrelatedness) are coalition-building leadership skills. I also emphasize coalition skills in our leadership development opportunities to highlight the importance of these skills. Drawing in others and developing relationships to create change have been vital to every organization individually and helpful in navigating their futures collectively.

Consider Visibility

In working with any student population, it is important to not only assess who is present but also who is absent. In the same way that Keating (2013) encourages listening with raw openness for what is and is not said, student affairs educators must scan our environments for who is and is not present. Once identified, we need to ask why this is the case and what can be done to create opportunities for the people not present. How might we understand students' experiences holistically? How can we consider students and the complex intersections of their identities? If I only see cis-women students engage in my office's programming, I need to ask questions about why I am not seeing cis-men and nonbinary students and change my communication and outreach approaches accordingly.

The same is true regarding what communication we release and what activities we plan. The APIMEDA Programs and Services office staff and I think about how we represent the people we serve and how we are talking about who is being included. We also think about who has not been represented and how we can consciously find ways to increase their representation in our displays of history and in our events. Regularly, we have heard from students that this attentiveness to representation and inclusion matters to them. Sometimes our office is the only place on campus where they feel seen. And the goal for my office is to help more students feel seen in more places.

CONCLUSION

Creating the APIMEDA Programs and Services office at UC San Diego has taught me to be more intentional about how I choose to communicate with not only the student populations with whom I work, but also campus partners. Embracing the complexities of how students' experiences are connected and different has allowed me to better understand the needs of my students and be a better advocate for their needs. I have the honor of watching them build strong communities and coalitions. And I look forward to continuing to listen to them describe their experiences and their needs as more students connect with my office.

REFERENCES

Ahmadi, S., & Cole, D. (2020). *Islamophobia in higher education: Combating discrimination and creating understanding.* Stylus.

Chang, M. J. (2011). Asian American and Pacific Islander millennial students at a tipping point. In F. A. Bonner II, A. F. Marbley, & M. F. Howard-Hamilton (Eds.), *Diverse millennial students in college: Implications for faculty and student affairs* (pp. 55–67). Stylus.

Coalition for Critical Asian American Studies. (2014, February 26). *Open letter.* https://apimeda.ucsd.edu/_files/ccaas-open-letter.pdf

Empowering Pacific Islander Communities & Asian Americans Advancing Justice. (2014). *A community of contrasts: Native Hawaiians and Pacific Islanders in California.* https://www.empoweredpi.org/uploads/1/1/4/1/114188135/a_community_of_contrasts_nhpi_ca_2014_low-res1.pdf

Espiritu, Y. L. (1992). *Asian American panethnicity: Bridging institutions and identities.* Temple University Press.

Kambhampaty, A. P. (2020, May 22). In 1968, these activists coined the term "Asian American" and helped shape decades of advocacy. *Time.* https://time.com/5837805/asian-american-history/?fbclid=IwAR0K3yp1U_3nm725ErBt7I aiXjaHxjmG25V6YyUBaMfs7Cytw-ul56fG9LQ

Keating, A. (2013). *Transformation now! Toward a post-oppositional politics of change.* University of Illinois Press.

Kim, C. J. (1999). The racial triangulation of Asian Americans. *Politics & Society, 27*(1), 105–138. https://doi.org/10.1177/0032329299027001005

Merriam-Webster. (n.d.). *Coalition.* Merriam-Webster.com dictionary. Retrieved May 10, 2022 from https://www.merriam-webster.com/

Merriam-Webster. (n.d.). *Community*. Merriam-Webster.com dictionary. Retrieved May 10, 2022 from https://www.merriam-webster.com/

Shotton, H. J., Lowe, S. C., & Watterman, S. J. (2013). Introduction. In H. J. Shotton, S. C. Lowe, & S. J. Watterman (Eds.), *Beyond the asterisk: Understanding Native students in higher education* (pp. 1–24). Stylus.

The Campaign for College Opportunity. (2015, September). *The state of higher education in California-Asian American, Native Hawaiian, Pacific Islander report.* https://collegecampaign.org/wp-content/uploads/2015/09/2015-State-of-Higher-Education_AANHPI2.pdf

University of California Information Center. (n.d.a). *Disaggregated data.* https://www.universityofcalifornia.edu/infocenter/disaggregated-data

University of California Information Center. (n.d.b). *Fall enrollment at a glance.* https://www.universityofcalifornia.edu/infocenter/fall-enrollment-glance

University of California San Diego, Office of Equity, Diversity, and Inclusion. (n.d.). *Undergraduate diversity dashboard.* https://diversity.ucsd.edu/accountability/undergrad.html

University of California San Diego, Office of Institutional Research. (n.d.). *Student profile 2019–2020.* https://ir.ucsd.edu/undergrad/publications/19_20_Student-Profile.pdf

University of California San Diego, Student Retention Services. (n.d.). *Defining the population.* https://srs.ucsd.edu/support/underserved.html#Defining-the-Population

Watt, S. K. (2015). *Designing transformative multicultural initiatives: Theoretical foundations, practical applications, and facilitator considerations.* Stylus.

Wiltz, T. (2014, August 13). *Counting Americans of Middle Eastern, North African descent.* Pew. https://www.pewtrusts.org/en/research-and-analysis/blogs/stateline/2014/08/13/counting-americans-of-middle-eastern-north-african-descent

10

Missed Connections

The Complicated Nature of Listening

Kia Rivera and Michelle Wallace

"THERE IS NO SUCH thing as a single-issue struggle, because we do not live single issue lives" (Lorde, 1982, p. 138). Many of us have heard or read this Audre Lorde quote from her address "Learning From the 60s," and still, the complicated reality of this quote rings true in our lived experiences and movements toward understanding and collective liberation.

In this chapter we highlight the ethical considerations of applying identity interconnections in practice in ways that do not perpetuate concepts of intersectional erasure (Abes & Wallace, 2018), or reduction to a single identity/single-issue being, through our own personal narratives of missed identity connections. Moreover, we use the lessons learned from our narratives as a catalyst toward developing deep identity interconnections within student affairs practice through intergroup dialogue. We explore the complexities and power that can be found through identity interconnections by expanding on the compassionate caution outlined by Keating's (2013) statement, "Denying the differences doesn't bring us together; it pushes us further apart" (p. 44). Furthermore, we explore intergroup dialogue as a facilitative tool to develop an ability to listen with "raw openness" and a "willingness to posit and seek commonalities defined not as sameness but as intertwined differences and possible points of connection" (Keating, 2013, p. 54).

155

Due to our own identities, we center our narratives around the concepts of "passing" (misunderstanding or nondisclosure of identity; both unintentional and purposeful) and "coming out" (purposeful disclosure of identity) in our given communities as sites of the violence that occurs when we, or those around us, are unwilling to listen with raw openness to not only the similarities but the differences across identity resulting in intersectional erasure. Erving Goffman (as cited in Silvermint, 2018) defines passing as a strategy aimed at "the management of undisclosed discrediting information about the self," or the kind of information that marks someone as a member of a different, less desirable category, reducing them in others' minds from a normal person to a "tainted, discounted one" (p. 2). According to Whaley (2018), "for a person to pass for an identity unlike the one socially ascribed, the viewer of the person must hold essentialist ideas about what constitutes and looks like a given identity" (p. 194). Passing then results in a marginalized individual having to choose what aspects of themselves they are willing to, or able to, share in a context where they are misread and placed within a norm, thus creating a tumultuous site for missed identity interconnection:

> To pass as [W]hite was to make an anxious decision to leave one racial identity and to claim to belong to another. It was risky business. In today's multiracial society, the decision to pass may seem foolish, frivolous, or disloyal. (Hobbs, 2018, p. 134)

The concept of "coming out" exists then as a response to the concept of "passing;" in other words, to "come out" is to reject socially ascribed (dominant) norms.

While the term "coming out" was popularized within LGBTQ rights movements as a tool to build solidarity and visibility (Saguy, 2020), and "passing" gained its origins in horrific descriptions of escaped slaves (Hobbs, 2018), these terms can be extended to similar experiences of many in marginalized communities that face definition and misreading by dominant groups. This point is further clarified by Hobbs (2018),

> Racial passing in the American context must be acknowledged as a subset of a much larger phenomenon. The poor passed as the rich, women passed as men, Jews passed as Gentiles, gay men and women passed as straight, and whites sometimes passed as black. (p. 134)

Within (dis)ability, lesbian, gay, bisexual, transgender, queer+, Black and non-Black Person of Color (POC) communities (among others), the need for "coming out" or disclosures and "passing" is very much an act of survival when living in a society full of hegemonic norms. Keating (2013) explains this reality exists because we live in a heteronormative, White supremacist society, which in turn develops these concepts as different results and responses to a larger systemic misreading or assumed norm.

While these similarities open opportunities for empathy building across experience, they also create a dangerous pitfall that highlights the need for compassionate caution that must be taken when forging identity interconnections. This pitfall exists within the danger of not acknowledging the unique histories, context, and implications that exist for those who hold multiple intersections of coming out and passing across differing identities. The conditions, which often result in missing the unique ways history and context impact one's narrative, manifest when we do not listen openly with the intent to be changed (Keating, 2013). For example, not being careful to recognize these differences can result in the erasure of experiences and consequences. Crenshaw (1989) defines intersectional erasure as the invisibility that results from interconnected multiple oppressed identities. Further expanded on by Abes and Wallace (2018), intersectional erasure often results in an individual being hyper-visible or objectified (standing out but never being seen as more than just that identity). An identity is viewed as additive and not intersectional or applicable to other experiences; this gaze may force an individual to make the difficult and detrimental choice of downplaying an identity to survive within a given community space.

NARRATIVES OF MISSED CONNECTIONS

Identity interconnections create opportunities for building understanding and connectedness across differences. Yet these connections can only happen if folks are able to acknowledge their differences in ways that allow for learning and not harm. We leverage our narratives and implications for practice to manifest cautionary tales around the way in which harm can be perpetuated within *missed* identity connections. Our examples explore themes of inability to truly listen due to assumptions around shared experiences or willful ignorance of differences even within an affinity community. Our narratives as a queer, non-(dis)abled, Womxn of Color, and a queer, (dis)abled, White womxn highlight moments in our lives that could have been transformed by identity interconnections but instead resulted in intersectional erasure and perpetuation of harm due to the inability of others to listen. We examine these narratives as a call to action when it comes to the student affairs field to ensure that this intersectional erasure does not continue.

Kia's Narrative

Constantly needing to navigate queer spaces as a Queer Person of Color has been exhausting because I either choose a salient identity or push back on queer spaces that center whiteness. In queer spaces, the lack of overall openness when it comes to identity interconnections has left me feeling a sense of loss within both personal and professional communities to which I belong. From my personal experience, the idea of making connections with others within the LGBTQA+ has proven difficult due to the lack of acknowledgement of racism within the LGBTQA+ community. The persistent need to prove that I am worthy of being in a space regardless of my race/ethnic identity is an example of intersectional erasure.

Consistently, queer spaces center whiteness in culture, narrative, and leadership; we can see this around the country within LGBTQA+ resource centers, LGBTQA+ student organizations, LGBTQA+ staff affinity groups, and so on. It happens in major cities, at pride parades, and even in how mainstream media depicts queerness. For me, the erasure of People of Color within the LGBTQA+ community shows up at all levels. LGBTQA+ celebrities tend to be White, pride parades tend to be White, there are very few Queer, Trans, People Of Color (QTPOC) bars or clubs, and even the LGBTQA+ history we learn about tends to be through a White lens, which continues to cause harm by erasing QTPOC communities from important narratives. It also creates the dynamic in which whiteness is centered as the default or the norm within LGBTQ+ communities and spaces.

Continually in my professional career, I have been expected to choose what identity—my race or my sexuality—I have wanted to be most salient in a space. This has also been true in most of my personal life but has become more apparent as I continue my career within higher education. In Black and non-Black POC spaces, I am often one of a few QTPOC folks and often feel as though I have to hide my queerness in order to not continuously be othered. I am often at a loss for how I can hold my Black and non-Black POC siblings to a standard of including LGBTQA+ identities while also trying to fight anti-Black racism in the queer community.

In particular, when conducting trainings on race and racism, it is often my White LGBTQA+ colleagues who have a hard time understanding how they play into a White supremacist culture and often make their experiences with homophobia the discussion. When this occurs, it is clear to me that they do not want to take the time to fully employ identity interconnections as a way to learn from and about each other. They are unable to do the hard work of being a true ally, which includes listening even when it is not easy. Instead, they choose to fold themselves into the conversation in a way that ends up erasing my experiences. Had these folks listened with the intent of being changed or listened with raw openness (Keating, 2013) a lot of the pain and erasure I have felt could have been avoided. One example of this erasure was when a cisgender, White gay male colleague took a training into his own hands. During every debrief in our small group, he took up so much space and was unable to see how he too played into and benefited from a White supremacist society. Despite my labor and multiple attempts to show examples of how White supremacy exists within the LGBTQA+ community, this group member missed the chance to see how he was also playing a role in continuing to perpetuate this culture. His inability to listen and acknowledge the lived experience that I shared silenced me and minimized the experiences of others within the group, thereby recentering whiteness in the workshop. I did not know if I could show up in the discussion as a fellow Queer person or a non-Black Person of Color. It felt like a critical betrayal from someone within a community I thought would "get it"; however, it caused me more harm and made me want to distance myself from the queer community professionally.

While my White colleagues tend to have difficulty challenging the idea of racism within the LGBTQA+ community, I also see homophobia play out within Black and non-Black POC spaces. When in spaces with Black and non-Black POC, I feel as though I can only be a Person of Color and that my queerness has no space within my narrative as we cannot focus on how homophobia comes into these spaces. I, for one, thought that within Black and non-Black POC spaces, I could finally be my full self, but that is not always the case. It is not always safe or comfortable for me to "come out" as a queer woman. This is something I continue to struggle with in professional spaces as I do not want my queerness to somehow undermine me as a non-Black POC.

Michelle's Narrative

All too often when searching for community, particularly surrounding my queer and (dis)abled identities, I find myself faced with an impossible decision: show up authentically and be marginalized within the community

I seek, or downplay and choose not to disclose an identity and find support around a single facet of myself. The intersection of my queer and (dis)abled identities has always been a complicated one for me. When entering (dis)abled community spaces, I often feel my Queer identity being erased either by the systemic erasing of sexuality among (dis)abled communities in general, the consistent mistaking a partner for a caregiver, or my own fear of marginalization within an already hard-to-find community.

A salient example of this for me was when I attended a conference about LGBTQ identity and activism. When given this opportunity, I was filled with the excitement of truly finding a home and belonging in the community and for myself. When I arrived, this was far from the truth. I found myself facing incredible pushback around my (dis)abled identity (which at times was visible and at others was not). One of my first experiences upon entering the conference was standing at the accessibility table to get a large print conference guide and being completely ignored. When I finally confronted the person at the table, I heard them whisper, "I didn't think she could see that I was standing here," referencing the white cane that I had been using at the time. This wasn't a one-off microaggression. Throughout my time at the conference, I was physically handled by passersby so that I would be "out of their way" for elevator access, accused of faking my disability because I wore glasses and had some sight, and unable to see presentations in packed rooms where I was often told to sit in the back and just listen.

Throughout my time within that space, I often found myself contemplating whether I would be better off putting away my cane and not disclosing my disabilities. This choice would mean not only denying a part of myself but also risking falling on uneven surfaces and access to conference materials in a format that allows me to fully contribute. However, it would grant me access to being seen as knowledgeable and valuable within the space. I spent much of my time grappling with this choice, a choice I knew other (dis)abled folks did not necessarily have to negotiate due to the visibility of their identities.

I was tired, hurt, and angry at the injustice that non-(dis)abled queer individuals not only were perpetuating ableism in a space I so longed to call home, but that on top of creating that culture, non-(dis)abled people in the space did not have to hold the labor of these choices. Something about this particular experience felt more painful and weighed heavier on my mind than the daily microaggressions that I felt in other spaces. Even as I reflect here in this chapter, I feel tension in my body and mind as I write.

Analysis

Our narratives manifest the pitfall of how relating through a singular under-standing of identity does not equate, and often counteracts, the ability to listen openly in order to develop identity interconnectedness. Instead of effectively employing identity interconnections, we experienced intersec-tional erasure, and it harmed everyone despite often good intentions. These concepts showed up for us in different ways across our narratives. Even in this analysis, we grapple with the similarities in inherited systems of power that otherize us and force us to choose a singular identity, which evoke unique history, consequences, and reactions that impact our navigation of and resist-ance to identity erasure.

Kia's Analysis

Within my example of this narrative of my White LGBTQA+ colleagues, intersectional erasure is clear when a conversation intended to examine race continues to come back to homophobia. Along with my experiences of "coming out" or choosing not to be within Black and non-Black POC spaces, I have always felt a need to choose one identity over the other. The oversimplification that homophobia and racism are inherently the same without acknowledging the presence of other identities does not allow for multitudes of truths. Along with the need and/or feeling of having to hide queerness when with Black and non-Black POC, it does not allow for others to come into the space and share their narratives or lived experiences. I argue that in these scenarios, identity interconnections did not occur, nor did social justice action happen.

One would think finding similarities in which we are all misread, defined, and othered by dominant systems would be a site for building empathy, and in some ways, it is. However, often noting these similarities falls short of examining the harder and more nuanced ways that our oppressions operate differently, such that we can work toward intergroup solidarity. Addressing antiracism and anti-Blackness in queer spaces may require folks to look inward rather than outward. Similarly, Black and non-Black POC spaces may need to engage difficult conversations around inclusion of LGBTQA+ identities.

Sometimes even when individuals hold similar social identities (in our example both holding LGBTQ identities), there seems to be a lack of understanding about the ways in which other marginalized identities (in our example our racial identities) transform experiences of oppression (homophobia). Not allowing space for this complexity when building that understanding often perpetuates pain and mistrust within our shared communities. Specifically, when folks hold dominant or privileged identities within a space and are unable to understand how their power takes up in spaces even in marginalized communities, they turn to their most salient oppressed identity rather than listening with raw openness (Keating, 2013) in such a way that allows for a coming together despite any differences. From my experience LGBTQA+ people tend to look at how others have harmed them rather than examining how they may have potentially caused harm to others. This makes it hard to conduct trainings on race and racism when White folks center their LGBTQA+ experiences instead of looking at how they may perpetuate racism and benefit from White supremacy.

Michelle's Analysis

After a lot of reflection . . . and therapy, I have come to understand why the harm that I felt in the example I shared previously continued to feel so salient to me; it was the missed opportunity of finding identity interconnectedness. Being both queer and (dis)abled, I expected that those within the queer community would make connections to the concepts of fluidity, visibility of an identity, and the complexities of having to disclose identity in order to feel whole in a space or, in my case, even be able to access and participate in a space. In short, I assumed that those who had faced similar forms of marginalization would operate from the framework of not perpetuating that marginalization with the privileged identities that they held. My hope is that this assumption is not completely untrue. Instead, the missing piece was the knowledge of how to listen with raw openness, beyond similarities in experience, to the experience of those at the margins of the margins and transform empathy into action.

The following year I chose to engage in that space again, this time with a clearer purpose, as I had connected with other queer, (dis)abled participants who had also faced ableism within the conference. We spent much of our time in affinity space crafting a list of demands and experiences to present to the conference board in the hopes of developing a space that was inclusive of the diverse identities within the queer community. Our presentation resulted in many empathetic tears from members of the board and heartfelt apologies; however, in continuing to engage with the space, very little changed. The empathy with our pain did not result in systemic or cultural change within the space nor move anyone toward accountability. The unrealized assumption that intersectional identities would be embraced holistically (and not additively)—acknowledging and exploring unique implications and consequences—resulted in incredible harm on all sides. When working toward the development of identity interconnections, there must be clear intentionality, compassionate caution, and a willingness to engage differences and intersecting areas of dominance. Student affairs educators must be ready to grapple with the complicated ways that we are all socialized to perpetuate power, and thus may cause harm, and be willing to draw expansive connections (inclusive of differences) across experience to pursue collective liberation.

Making Meaning

Both of our narratives center around missed identity interconnections due to the inability to listen with raw openness, which resulted in intersectional erasure. Our examples highlight the ways in which inherited systems of power result in norms that otherize us; that force us to deny a part of ourselves (to pass) in order to gain access, or to resist the norm and risk losing access through disclosure or coming out. Whether it is deciding to request an accommodation, to wear natural hair, to correct someone on the pronouns of a partner, or countless other examples, instances of societal norms instigating the need to survive either within the norms (passing) or resisting them (coming out) go far beyond what is shared previously. This is a systemic issue that results in the onus landing on an individual and develops not only undue stress but, despite the ways that it presents across systems, complicates the ability to listen with raw openness.

In Kia's narrative her colleague's inability to recognize and develop understanding around the unique consequences when one is resisting or surviving within by navigating "coming out" or "passing" (e.g., what one gets access to when passing as straight or cisgender is different than what one gets access to when passing for White) perpetuated a single-issue understanding of LBGTQ identity. Whether this was done in an attempt to build empathy in recognizing sameness, or to avoid confronting the more nuanced conversation about holding privilege within a marginalized community, it impacted Kia's colleague's ability to listen to Kia's experiences and resulted in a missed identity interconnection. Moreover, this issue was further exacerbated because it left Kia feeling a sense of intersectional erasure within her communities (e.g., never feeling fully a part of the queer community or non-Black POC community). That broke the trust needed to develop meaningful interconnections.

Similarly, Michelle's narrative highlighted a moment where listening with raw openness and intentionality could have transformed an experience of feeling othered into one of systemic change. Those who held power within the marginalized community expressed guilt for a community being oppressed but did not seek the connection as to the ways in which queer liberation and disability justice are intertwined. In the words of Mia Mingus (2011), "Ableism is connected to all of our struggles because it undergirds notions of whose bodies are considered valuable, desirable and disposable" (para. 18). There was a conflict of intentionality that created difficulty on all sides to listen. In an all-too-rare space that centers marginalized experiences, there was no unified intentionality to develop the ability to listen and effectively engage identity interconnections. Instead, there were a multitude of expectations and intentions across the many communities within that space.

Keating (2013) states the following, "Interconnectivity and interrelatedness: What affects others—*all* others, no matter how separate we seem to be ultimately affects [us] as well" (p. 23). Identity interconnections can contribute to solidarity building through understanding when, how, and why these moments of "other'" show up for different communities and can allow action as accomplices across difference and a common call for change. Our two narratives serve as cautionary tales of just how easy it can be to miss an opportunity to meet one another's humanity with intention and raw openness, resulting in harm and missed identity interconnections.

IMPLICATIONS FOR PRACTICE

In the previous section, we offer some examples of missed identity interconnections that highlight the compassionate caution needed to listen not only for similarities in our collective struggles, but also to do the hard and transformative work of listening to understand the differences in the historical contexts, ways of being, and consequences of being. Within both of our examples, the pitfall (or missed opportunity) was in failing to listen with the intent of being changed (Keating, 2013). We often listen with the intention of understanding another only to the extent necessary to form our own reaction or response. When this happens, we run the risk of minimizing differences and missing the transformative possibilities for social justice action that identity interconnections can offer. If we instead take what Keating (2013) writes about regarding listening with raw openness, and apply it to the previous examples, missed identity interconnections would not occur. These examples hold important implications for student affairs educators who are working toward justice alongside their students.

One facilitative tool which we would like to offer is intergroup dialogue. Intergroup dialogue allows students and educators alike to develop the capacity to listen with raw openness in order to foster identity interconnections and pursue collective liberation. Intergroup dialogue is a facilitated experience that allows students, faculty, and staff to communicate and build understanding across social division with the goals of

> [P]romoting the development of consciousness about social identity and social group difference . . . helping members of social identity groups with a history of conflict or personal conflict to forge connections across differences . . . and strengthening individual and collective capacities for social action by fostering connections across identity groups. (Zúñiga et al., 2007, p. viii)

Through intergroup dialogue, participants have the opportunity to engage not only in understanding the similarities across experience but also examining how social identity uniquely manifests for different identity groups and how they can work together to show up as allies. In other words, intergroup dialogue enhances the complexity of a participant's meaning-making filter (Abes et al., 2007). The opportunity to set intentions and build relationships within intergroup communities allows participants to see similarities across inherited systems of power and build empathy, as well as to unpack the ways in which they might be perpetuating similar systems within dominant identities that they hold. Listening without the intent to be changed (Keating, 2013) causes harm within the communities in which we are seeking refuge. Thus, holding intergroup dialogue space may help to resolve barriers to listening through fostering intentional community commitment to develop identity interconnections, as well as accountability by calling into conversation moments that create intersectional erasure.

Additionally, student affairs educators should view themselves and their own liberation as tied to the liberation of their students. As Ashlee and Combs explain in the introduction (this volume), practicing building the capacity to listen with raw openness means listening with the intent to be changed and challenged. This can happen within all facets of our work. Examples of this might include practicing intergroup dialogue as a participant along-side students; building intergroup dialogue into departmental culture, job descriptions, and values exercises; and engaging in training and professional development opportunities. As a result of this work, we believe that a rich and engaging understanding of the interconnectedness between student affairs educators and student experiences will arise along with a newfound mastery of student-centered listening and acting as an ally or accomplice in transforming the landscape of higher education toward justice. When we talk about allyship and being an accomplice, we use the terms as a call to action. Being an ally is a verb, and a continuous cycle in which we constantly are learning, growing, and challenging ourselves to show up for those around us (Love, 2020). Being an accomplice means we are using our power and privilege to challenge inherited systems of power (Love, 2020).

CONCLUSION

In her *Disability Justice Is Simply Another Term for Love* blog post, Mia Mingus (2018) writes,

> I don't just want us to get a seat at someone else's table, I want us to be able to build something more magnificent than a table, together with our accomplices. I want us to be able to be understood and to be able to take part in principled struggle together—to be able to be *human* together. Not just placated or politely listened to. (para. 24)

This goal is long and difficult, and it starts and develops with the capacity to listen, to build empathy for our collective struggle, and to act where we can against inequities across differences.

While our narratives may differ, we can agree that some of our most profound experiences when it comes to this work have been experienced during intergroup dialogue work. These have been some of the most meaningful conversations with colleagues and students and have led us to feeling seen within our full humanity and continue to call us into learning how to listen with raw openness to those around us. To truly work toward collective liberation, we desperately need the perspectives and participation from people across communities. Identity interconnections offer a unique opportunity to work against intersectional erasure, which perpetuates the creation of the table and who is seated at it. Instead, these connections invite us to explore the importance of listening to be changed, working toward building something more magnificent than the table.

REFERENCES

Abes, E. S., Jones, S. R., & McEwen, M. K. (2007). Reconceptualizing the model of multiple dimensions of identity: The role of meaning-making capacity in the construction of multiple identities. *Journal of College Student Development, 48*(1), 1–22. https://doi.org/10.1353/csd.2007.0000

Abes, E. S., & Wallace, M. M. (2018). "People see me, but they don't see me": An intersectional study of college students with physical disabilities. *Journal of College Student Development, 59*(5), 545–562. https://doi.org/10.1353/csd.2018.0052

Berne, P. (2015, June 10). *Disability justice—a working draft.* http://sinsinvalid.org/blog/disability-justice-a-working-draft-by-patty-berne

Crenshaw, K. (1989). Demarginalizing the intersection of race and sex: A Black feminist critique of antidiscrimination doctrine, feminist theory, and antiracist politics. *University of Chicago Legal Forum, 8*(1), 139–167. https://chicagounbound.uchicago.edu/uclf/vol1989/iss1/8

Hancock, A. (2011). *Solidarity politics for millennials: A guide to ending the oppression olympics.* Palgrave Macmillan.

Hobbs, A. (2018). Passing. In E. Edwards, R. Ferguson, & J. Ogbar (Eds.), *Keywords for African American studies* (pp. 133–135). NYU Press.

Keating, A. (2013). *Transformation now! Toward a post-oppositional politics of change.* University of Illinois Press. www.jstor.org/stable/10.5406/j.ctt3fh5zv

Lorde, A. (1982). *Sister outsider.* Crossing Press.

Love, A. (2020, September 9). *Allies, accomplices, and saviors: Knowing the difference to maximize impact.* Berrett-Koehler Publishers. https://ideas.bkconnection.com/allies-accomplices-saviors-knowing-the-difference-to-maximize-impact

Mingus, M. (2011, February 12). Changing the framework: Disability justice. How our communities can move beyond access to wholeness. *Leaving Evidence.* https://leavingevidence.wordpress.com/2011/02/12/changing-the-framework-disability-justice/

Mingus, M. (2018, November 3). Disability justice is simply another term for love. *Leaving Evidence.* https://leavingevidence.wordpress.com/2018/11/03/disability-justice-is-simply-another-term-for-love/

Ridder, S., & Dhaenens, F. (2019). Coming out as popular media practice: The politics of queer youth coming out on YouTube. *DiGeSt. Journal of Diversity and Gender Studies, 6*(2), 43–60. https://www.jstor.org/stable/10.11116/digest.6.2.3

Saguy, A. C. (2020). *Come out, come out, whoever you are.* Oxford University Press.

Silvermint, D. (2018). Passing as privileged. *Ergo, 5*(1). https://doi.org/10.3998/ergo.12405314.0005.001

Whaley, D. (2018). Neo-passing and dissociative identities as affective strategies in Frankie and Alice. In M. Godfrey & V. Young (Eds.), *Neo-passing: Performing identity after Jim Crow* (pp. 193–218). University of Illinois Press.

Zúñiga, X., Nagda, B. A., Chesler, M., & Cytron-Walker, A. (Eds.). (2007). Intergroup dialogue in higher education: Meaningful learning about social justice [Special issue]. *ASHE Higher Education Report, 32*(4).

Afterword

DISTINCT FROM AN EPILOGUE, which tells what happens to the characters in a fictional story after a book has ended, an afterword is often included in reprinted or subsequent versions of a nonfiction book to describe its lasting impact. I write my afterword while this book is initially going to press in anticipation of the possibilities it has to impact students' lives. I also think about this afterword in relation to an epilogue; that is, I write it knowing that educators cannot predict what will happen to the students after their college story has ended, but that they do influence the direction in significant ways. Guided by Aeriel and Lisa, the chapter authors in this book set a stage for liberatory practice that will contribute to rich, evolving student stories.

I was fortunate to have been in community with Aeriel and Lisa when they were graduate students at Miami University. I was one of their faculty members and appreciated learning with them as they individually explored the fluidity, multiplicity, and border-defying nature of their own identities and also as they forged a professional and personal relationship rooted in their identity interconnections. I witnessed the self-understanding and resolve they drew from these interconnections in an educational system that tends to define and create boundaries around identities, often resulting in erasure and self-doubt. In their self-understanding and resolve, I witnessed the conception of this book. I also realized my own need to continue doing better in how I apply third-wave student development theory in practice and how I teach others to do the same. This book offers useful insights on how to do so and will be one of its lasting impacts.

Specifically, this book resonates with my perception that college will be a more liberatory experience for historically erased students if student affairs practitioners embrace connection, fluidity, border crossing, and deep knowledge and understanding across differences. These ideas are consistent with the third wave of student development theory, and the ideas proposed in this book contribute to third-wave practice. Developed mostly by minoritized scholars, third-wave theory centers and resists intersecting systems of oppression, uplifting students who have been problematized and erased. Applying these theories in practice is especially urgent, and identity interconnections offer a framework for doing so.

A key aspect of practice starts with how the practitioner views the student. Dave Kasch, who coauthored an early third-wave student development article with me, described practice in relationship to how a viewer of art sees a painting. A pointilist piece of art, for instance, is understood differently depending on how the viewer sees it. It is either a series of dots or it is a rich, detailed picture. When practitioners see identity interconnections across students rather than distinct boundaries—necessarily with the "compassionate caution" that Aeriel and Lisa urge to respect differences across identities—they can work against campus cultures that serve and center dominant populations of students. They can, for instance, hone in on microaggressions, sociopolitical conditions, silence, and the development of allies and coconspirators. Practitioners can recognize that a lack of expertise must not stop them from acting on behalf of particular students as long as they commit to deep learning. Practitioners can more effectively nurture coalitions and purposeful spaces for multiple historically marginalized students and also individual homes—and understand the need for both.

Riding the values of the profession, student affairs educators often claim an understanding of identity and systems of oppression when they (we) still have so much to learn, resulting in harm. We all must acknowledge how much we have to learn about each other (and ourselves). Aeriel, Lisa, and the chapter authors are pushing us to learn more deeply through identity interconnectivity. When put into practice well—with a respect for both connections and differences—students will experience more liberatory college environments. I look forward to the lasting impact that these experiences will have on their evolving stories.

Elisa S. Abes
Miami University
Oxford, Ohio

Editors and Contributors

EDITORS

AERIEL A. ASHLEE (she/her), PhD, is an assistant professor and graduate program director of the college counseling and student development master's program at St. Cloud State University (SCSU). She is also the SCSU Center for Excellence in Teaching and Learning Belonging Mindset Faculty Fellow. Her teaching, scholarship, and activism are guided by her desire and commitment to facilitate healing and liberation in higher education. Prior to becoming faculty, Aeriel had a decade-long career in student affairs. Her research interests include critical autoethnography as transformative methodology, poststructural possibilities for student affairs praxis, and the racialized experiences of underrepresented Asian Americans in higher education (specifically transracial adoptees and Hmong Americans). Along with peer-reviewed journal articles and book chapters, she is the coauthor of an award-winning book on social justice pedagogy.

LISA DELACRUZ COMBS (she/her/hers) is currently a doctoral student at The Ohio State University in the higher education and student affairs program. Prior to Ohio State, she was a program coordinator in the Student Diversity and Multicultural Affairs Office at Loyola University Chicago. Prior to working at Loyola University Chicago, she also worked as a coordinator for Campus Life at the Illinois Institute of Technology and as a graduate assistant in the Office of Community Engagement and Service at Miami University of Ohio. Lisa's research interests include identity interconnections, multiraciality in higher education, Filipinx identity development, and deconstructing social constructs around race. She has been published in the *Journal of College Student Development* and also served as the cochair for the

Multiracial Network in ACPA. She received her BA in political science and English from The Ohio State University and her MS in student affairs in higher education from Miami University in Oxford Ohio.

CONTRIBUTORS

ELISA S. ABES (she/her), PhD, is a professor in the Miami University student affairs in higher education program. Her research centers on critical theoretical approaches to student development theory, such as intersectionality, critical disability theory, and crip theory. She uses these theories to reimagine student development theory in ways that work against systems of inequality such as racism, ableism, and heterosexism. Elisa's current research focuses on the experiences and identities of college students with disabilities. Elisa is coeditor (with Susan R. Jones and D-L Stewart) of *Rethinking College Student Development Theory Using Critical Frameworks* (Stylus, 2019); editor of *Critical Perspectives on Student Development Theory* (Jossey Bass, 2016); and coauthor (with Susan R. Jones) of *Identity Development of College Students: Advancing Frameworks for Multiple Dimensions of Identity* (Jossey Bass, 2013). Elisa graduated from The Ohio State University with her bachelor's degree (1992) and doctorate (2003). She received her law degree from Harvard Law School (1995).

KYLE C. ASHLEE, PhD, teaches in the college counseling and student development master's program at St. Cloud State University. His research interests include critical whiteness studies, college men and masculinities, neoliberalism in higher education, and critical pedagogy. Kyle has authored several peer-reviewed journal articles and book chapters related to social justice in higher education, as well as an award-winning book on social justice pedagogy.

GENIA M. BETTENCOURT, PhD, is an assistant professor in higher and adult education at the University of Memphis and a research affiliate with the Pullias Center for Higher Education at the University of Southern California and the Center for Student Success Research at the University of Massachusetts Amherst. Her research centers questions of access, equity, and activism for marginalized student populations, particularly focusing on issues of social class. She holds a master's degree in college student services administration from Oregon State University and bachelor's degrees in English, history, and political science from the University of California Davis. Prior to beginning her doctoral program, Genia worked in student affairs across residence life, precollege programs, and student leadership.

HOA BUI (she/her/hers), MS, is currently an area coordinator in residence life and community development at La Salle University. Bui's journey in the student affairs world started with her involvement in activism at Colgate University, her alma mater. Receiving her master's from the student affairs and higher education program at Miami University of Ohio, Bui subsequently served as a resident director at Miami University. Passionate about decoloniality, transnational feminism, and international education, Bui has published several book chapters and journal articles on these topics.

KELLI CAMPA (she/her/hers) identifies as multiracial and interfaith, being half Hispanic and half White, as well as half Christian and half Jewish. Kelli grew up in Southern California but now calls the East Coast home. Kelli graduated with her bachelor's in communications and minored in religion from California Lutheran University. She graduated with her master's in higher education from Iowa State University. Kelli has worked within residential life, conferences and event services, learning communities, student life, orientation, and student conduct.

BRANDON CASH, MS, currently serves as the director of student activities at St. Olaf College. His research interests consist primarily of masculinity, meaningful student involvement, and the new- and continuing-student transition and experience within the context of institutions of higher education.

REBECCA CEPEDA (she/her/ella/siya) is a doctoral candidate in the higher education and student affairs program at The Ohio State University. She received her BA in political science with a minor in Chicana/o studies at the University of California, Los Angeles, and her MEd in educational counseling at the University of Southern California. Currently, Rebecca is a graduate research assistant for OSU's Office of Student Academic Success, Student Research Lab. Rebecca identifies as Mexipina and conducts research on multiraciality in higher education. Her other research interests include centering the experiences of People of Color and community college students in higher education.

ANTONIO DURAN (he/him), PhD, is an assistant professor in the higher and postsecondary education program at Arizona State University. Antonio's main research line involves using critical and poststructural epistemologies to complicate the study of college student development and identity. In particular, he leverages frameworks such as intersectionality, queer of color critique, and quare theory to contribute to research about queer and trans people of color. Antonio is also particularly interested in the epistemological, methodological, and theoretical challenges/possibilities that emerge when employing critical and poststructural schools of thought in researching college student identity.

ALANDIS A. JOHNSON (they/them/theirs), PhD, is a White, nonbinary/transgender queer cancer survivor, living with chronic autoimmune disease, as well as depression and anxiety. They work outside of student affairs and higher education, yet continue to publish work related to gender, sexuality, and disability, specifically using poststructural and critical epistemologies to complicate theories about student development, identity, and resistance/activism.

MARC P. JOHNSTON-GUERRERO, PhD, is associate chair of the Department of Educational Studies, an associate professor in the higher education and student affairs (HESA) program, and affiliate faculty in Asian American studies at The Ohio State University. His research focuses on race and multiraciality across changing contexts.

KAITY PRIETO (she/her/hers), PhD, is an assistant professor at the University of Southern Mississippi. She has experience teaching undergraduate and graduate coursework focused on qualitative research, as well as power, privilege, inequality, and their role in student development. Kaity has written and presented on the experiences of LGBTQ+ students, with a focus on bisexual, pansexual, and fluid student communities. Her current research explores bisexual+ undergraduate and graduate student identity negotiation.

KAMRIE J. RISKU (she/her/hers) serves as the coordinator for curriculum and partnerships in the office of Leadership and Community Service-Learning at the University of Maryland, College Park. She earned her Bachelor of Arts in Political Science from North Carolina State University and her Master of Education in Higher Education, Student Affairs, and International Education Policy at the University of Maryland, College Park. Kamrie's research interests include multiraciality in higher education and applying justice-oriented frameworks to develop engaged teaching pedagogies. She also serves as the awards cocoordinator for the ACPA Multiracial Network.

KIA RIVERA (she/her/hers) is a DEI facilitator at She+ Geeks Out, working with companies to bridge the gap between the culture organizations have and the one organizations want, working specifically on racial equity, diversity and inclusion programing and curriculum. Before She+ Geek Out, Kia was a partnerships manager at Hack.Diversity. She earned her bachelor's degree in history from Lasell College, and her master's from Suffolk University. Kia is passionate about education reform, access along with advocacy within the LGBTQ+ community, and our collective liberation.

WINDI N. SASAKI (she/they) serves as UC San Diego's inaugural associate director for Asian Pacific Islander Middle Eastern Desi American (APIMEDA) Programs and Services. She has a BA from UC San Diego and an MA from Indiana University of Pennsylvania. She has over 20 years of experience working with diverse communities in higher education, both in educational institutions and in leadership roles within ACPA. A consistent thread in her professional work has been advocacy for coalitions of people and working with people to find opportunities for collective action.

MICHELLE WALLACE (she/her/hers) is the assistant director of the LGBTQA Resource Center at Northeastern University and was the assistant director of leadership development and collaborative initiatives at the time of writing this chapter. Michelle earned her bachelor's degree in psychology from Suffolk University, and her master's in student affairs and higher education from Miami University. She is currently on the board of the Consortium of Higher Education LGBT Resource Professionals. Michelle roots her praxis in intersectional disability justice and views working against ableism as inextricably tied to uprooting intersecting systems of oppression; she also views her own liberation as bound to the liberation of her students.

Index

mind and body distinction within, 54

models about, 54–55

narrative regarding, 87–88

personal narrative regarding, 159–160, 162–163

social model of, 44

stigmatizing of, 63, 90–91

theoretical frameworks for, 61–62

disclosure

construct of, 21

contamination of, 113

defined, 84

empowerment through, 94

of gender, 58–59

narrative regarding, 87–89

need for, 85

processes of, 91

repetition within, 92

stigma regarding, 90–91

support through, 90

disconnectionist approach, 3

discrimination, 63, 102

drugs, pain management, 57–58

emotional fragility, 127–128, 130

empathy, 63, 110–111, 162–163

English as a second language (ESL), 40, 42

English language, 40, 44, 45

enoughness, 29, 35

entitlement, culture of, 123

exclusionary questions, within interconnected othering, 30–32

failure, 56, 60

Federal Application for Financial Student Aid (FAFSA), 90

first-generation students, 93

first wave of student development, 13, 16–17

fluidity, 63, 101. See also bisexual identity

foreigner stereotype, 139

formal theory, 20

gender

assumptions regarding, 58–59

asterisk use regarding, 67

as constructed identity, 53

disclosure of, 58–59

equity regarding, 129

identity development regarding, 69–70

as infinite category, 52

privilege within, 125

theories regarding, 53–56

GI Bill, 84

Hanukkah, 32

heterosexism, 101

higher education, history of, 83–84

Hillel, 32

identity

community building within, 110–111

empathy for, 110–111

ethical considerations for, 112–114

experience and, 124

exploration opportunities regarding, 110–111

formal spaces for, 110–111

as hyper-visible, 109

intersection of, 103

as invisible, 109

liminality within, 56

multiple dimensions of, 108–109

passing of, 110

salience, 124

See also specific identities

identity analogy, 2

identity connection, 43–47

identity development theories, 65

identity experiences, 2

identity interconnections

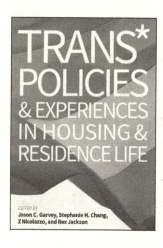

EDITED BY
Jason C. Garvey, Stephanie H. Chang,
Z Nicolazzo, and Rex Jackson

Trans* Policies & Experiences in Housing & Residence Life

Edited by Jason C. Garvey, Stephanie H. Chang, Z Nicolazzo, and Rex Jackson

Foreword by Kathleen G. Kerr

Copublished with ACPA

What are the institutional politics associated with fostering trans* inclusive policies? When formalizing a policy, what unanticipated challenges may emerge? How are students, particularly trans* students, influenced by the implementation of gender-inclusive housing practices and policies? Also, what are campus administrators and practitioners learning from their involvement with the development of trans* work on campus?

Housing and residence life (HRL) plays an important role in the safety, well-being, and sense of belonging for college students, but gender-inclusive policies and practices in HRL are largely under-explored in student affairs and higher education publications.

There are five key objectives that guide this book:

1. To promote and challenge student affairs and higher education staff knowledge about trans* students' identities and experiences;
2. To support and celebrate the accomplishments of educators and professionals in their strides to promote trans* inclusive policies and practices;
3. To highlight the unique role that housing and residence life plays in creating institutional change and serving trans* student populations;
4. To demonstrate the value and use of scholarly personal narratives, particularly for narrating experiences related to implementing trans* inclusive policies in housing and residence life; and
5. To create a strong partnership between scholarship and student affairs practice by developing an avenue for practitioner-scholars to publish their experiences related to gender-inclusive policies in housing and residence life and for others to use these stories to improve their practice.

Administrators, educators, and student affairs staff will find this book useful at any stage in the process of creating gender-inclusive housing policies on their campuses.

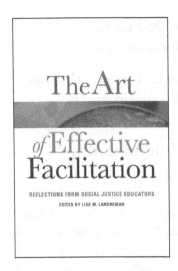

The Art of Effective Facilitation

Reflections From Social Justice Educators

Edited by Lisa M. Landreman

Copublished With ACPA

How can I apply learning and social justice theory to become a better facilitator?

Should I prepare differently for workshops around specific identities?

How do I effectively respond when things aren't going as planned?

This book is intended for the increasing number of faculty and student affairs administrators—at whatever their level of experience—who are being asked to become social justice educators to prepare students to live successfully within, and contribute to, an equitable multicultural society.

It will enable facilitators to create programs that go beyond superficial discussion of the issues to fundamentally address the structural and cultural causes of inequity and provide students with the knowledge and skills to work for a more just society. Beyond theory, design, techniques, and advice on practice, the book concludes with a section on supporting student social action.

The authors illuminate the art and complexity of facilitation, describe multiple approaches, and discuss the necessary and ongoing reflection process. What sets this book apart is how the authors illustrate these practices through personal narratives of challenges encountered, and by admitting to their struggles and mistakes.

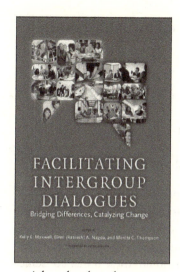

Facilitating Intergroup Dialogues

Bridging Differences, Catalyzing Change

Kelly E. Maxwell, Biren (Ratnesh) A. Nagda, and Monita C. Thompson

Foreword by Patricia Gurin

Copublished with ACPA

Intergroup dialogue has emerged as an effective educational and community-building method to bring together members of diverse social and cultural groups to engage in learning together so that they may work collectively and individually to promote greater diversity, equality, and justice.

Intergroup dialogues bring together individuals from different identity groups (e.g., people of color and white people; women and men; lesbian, gay, and bisexual people and heterosexual people), and uses explicit pedagogy that involves three important features: content learning, structured interaction, and facilitative guidance.

The least understood role in the pedagogy is that of facilitation. This volume, the first dedicated entirely to intergroup dialogue facilitation, draws on the experiences of contributors and on emerging research to address the multidimensional role of facilitators and cofacilitators, the training and support of facilitators, and ways of improving practice in both educational and community settings. It constitutes a comprehensive guide for practitioners, covering the theoretical, conceptual, and practical knowledge they need.

Multicultural Student Services on Campus

Building Bridges, Re-visioning Community

Edited by D-L Stewart

Copublished with ACPA

For new professionals in multicultural student services (MSS), this book constitutes a thorough introduction to the structure, organization, and scope of the services and educational mission of these units. For senior practitioners it offers insights for reevaluating their strategies and inspiration to explore new possibilities.

The book discusses the history and philosophy of MSS units; describes their operation; asserts the need for integration and coherence across the multiple facets of their work and how their role is influenced by the character and type of their institutions; and considers the challenges and opportunities ahead.

The theme Building Bridges, Re-Visioning Community reflects the dual role of MSS. They "build bridges" between underrepresented student populations and the broader institutional environment, between different groups of student populations, and across differences in cultural values and traditions. At a time of increasing diversity on campus, their role is also to champion the "re-visioning" or redefinition of what constitutes community in higher education—in other words to reach beyond serving their traditional constituencies to educate for multicultural competence and advocate for social justice across the campus commons.

Empowering Women in Higher Education and Student Affairs

Theory, Research, Narratives, and Practice From Feminist Perspectives

Edited by Penny A. Pasque and Shelley Errington Nicholson

Foreword by Linda J. Sax

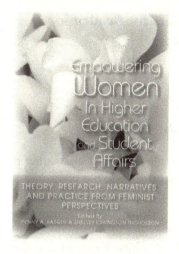

Copublished with

How do we interrupt the current paradigms of sexism in the academy? How do we construct a new and inclusive gender paradigm that resists the dominant values of the patriarchy? And why are these agendas important not just for women, but for higher education as a whole?

These are the questions that these extensive and rich analyses of the historical and contemporary roles of women in higher education—as administrators, faculty, students, and student affairs professionals—seek constructively to answer. In doing so they address the intersection of gender and women's other social identities, such as of race, ethnicity, sexual orientation, class, and ability.

This book addresses the experiences and position of women students, from application to college through graduate school, and the barriers they encounter; the continuing inequalities in the rates of promotion and progression of women and other marginalized groups to positions of authority, and the gap in earnings between men and women; and pays particular attention to how race and other social markers impact such disparities, contextualizing them across all institutional types.

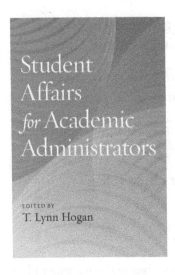

Student Affairs for Academic Administrators

Edited by T. Lynn Hogan

Copublished with

In these days when every college or university needs to make the best use of resources, *Student Affairs for Academic Administrators* is intended to help academic administrators make the best use of one vital campus resource: student affairs. By providing this concise introduction to student affairs as a discipline and a profession, the authors of this volume provide a foundation for working together to improve the student experience and enhance learning.

Since academic administrators typically come up through the faculty ranks, they are unlikely to have a good grasp of what their student affairs colleagues bring to the common work of education. To provide a better understanding, the chapters in this volume cover topics such as:

- the history of student affairs, and functions typically associated with student affairs divisions;
- current thinking and research in student development theory;
- theoretical constructs underlying contemporary student affairs practice (and ways to employ these theories in academic administration); and
- diversity issues and their impact on student outcomes in the collegiate environment.

After a chapter on how to build successful collaborations between academic affairs and student affairs, two final chapters explore specific examples of how such collaborations work in practice: academic honor codes, and undergraduate research. While written for academic administrators, the book also provides valuable insights for those in student affairs seeking to improve understanding and facilitate collaboration with colleagues in academic affairs.

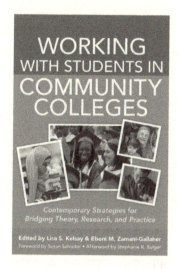

Working With Students in Community Colleges

Contemporary Strategies for Bridging Theory, Research, and Practice

Edited by Lisa S. Kelsay and Eboni M. Zamani-Gallaher

Foreword by Susan Salvador

Afterword by Stephanie R. Bulger

Copublished with

This timely volume addresses the urgent need for new strategies and better ways to serve community colleges' present and future students at a time of rapid diversification, not just racially and ethnically, but including such groups as the undocumented, international students, older adult learners and veterans, all of whom come with varied levels of academic and technical skills.

The contributing researchers, higher education faculty, college presidents, and community college administrators provide thorough understanding of student groups who have received scant attention in the higher education literature. They address the often unconscious barriers to access our institutions have erected and describe emerging strategies, frameworks, and pilot projects that can ease students' transition into college and through the maze of the college experience to completion.

Also available from Stylus

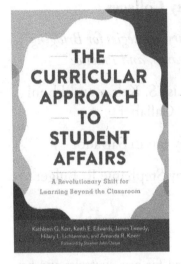

The Curricular Approach to Student Affairs

A Revolutionary Shift for Learning Beyond the Classroom

Kathleen G. Kerr, Keith E. Edwards, James Tweedy, Hilary L. Lichterman, and Amanda R. Knerr

Foreword by Stephen John Quaye

The curricular approach aligns the mission, goals, outcomes, and practices of a student affairs division, unit, or other unit that works to educate students beyond the classroom with those of the institution, and organizes intentional and developmentally sequenced strategies to facilitate student learning. In this book, the authors explain how to implement a curricular approach for educating students beyond the classroom. The book is based on more than a decade of implementing curricular approaches on multiple campuses, contributing to the scholarship on the curricular approach, and helping many campuses design, implement, and assess their student learning efforts. The curricular approach is rooted in scholarship and the connections between what we know about learning, assessment, pedagogy, and student success. For many who have been socialized in a more traditional programming approach, it may feel revolutionary. Yet, it is also obvious because it is straightforward and simple.

22883 Quicksilver Drive
Sterling, VA 20166-2019

Subscribe to our email alerts: www.Styluspub.com